THE PLIANT ANIMAL

THE PLIANT ANIMAL

Dr. George Weinberg

St. Martin's Press   New York

Library of Congress Cataloging in Publication Data

Weinberg, George H
    The pliant animal.

    1. Personality change.   2. Free will and
determinism.   3. Psychotherapy.   I. Title.
BF698.2.W43   158'.1   80-22486
ISBN 0-312-61751-8

Editor's Note

In my career as an editor, I have published somewhere in the neighborhood of 700 books, ranging from thrillers and literary fiction to medical and engineering volumes. This is the first time, though, I have asked an author to allow me to address a few words to the reader as a sort of introduction to his book.

The Pliant Animal is, I believe, an important book that will—if there is any justice in the world—live long after I have disappeared from the publishing scene. Dr. George Weinberg's themes are numerous, and in a fundamental sense simple and accessible. More to the point, his thinking is elegantly logical and eminently *sane*. What Dr. Weinberg says to us all, whether we be psychologists or laypersons, is that we are free, that free will and human dignity do exist, and that there are techniques virtually all of us can employ to help us understand ourselves and overcome the problems that all of us sooner or later must grapple with. This is a serious book that addresses serious issues, but I believe few readers will fail to notice the spirit of joy, even passion, that permeates the entire work. Some may disagree with one or another of Dr. Weinberg's conclusions, but I have little doubt that most of us who join him on this intellectual journey will find ourselves changed for the better.

Thomas L. Dunne
Executive Editor
St. Martin's Press

Acknowledgments

I would like to thank Barbara Warren for helping me organize and present these ideas, which are so important to me. And Tom Dunne, my editor at St. Martin's, for his many suggestions at every stage. And Dr. Alice Fennessey, for her many psychological insights and her suggestions about the writing of this book.

Table of Contents

Part Three: THE PRACTICAL SIDE OF PLIANCY

PART ONE
The Descent of Psychology

CHAPTER ONE

Human Pliancy

Across the animal kingdom, one finds almost every conceivable kind of behavior. Some animals, like wild dogs, live in a tight-knit unit, all for one and one for all. Others, like the leopard, spend virtually their entire adult lives alone. Wolves are monogamous, but most animals are not. Geese are faithful to their first loves, but if a first love dies, the goose is never faithful again. Most species, but not all, will care for their young. Animals differ in whether they are territorial, nomadic, aggressive or passive by nature, in whether they kill only for food, and in countless other ways.

Such distinguishing traits are often, if not always, crucial to the survival of the species. The traits themselves are predictable. Separate a member from others of its kind soon after birth, and at later stages it will show the characteristics of its particular species—as if it had a species "memory" and the necessity to display those qualities.

What distinguishes human beings from all other creatures is our incredible *pliancy*. There seems as much variety

among us as across the whole animal kingdom. Great numbers of people have lived in each of the ways mentioned.
Our pliancy, our ability to live under and become accustomed to diverse conditions, far exceeds that of any other
creature. Move the human child from its own society to
another early in life and it will behave like a perfect member of the new society. Adaptability is characteristic of the
human species in the same way that banding together is of
the wild dog and the wandering life is of the ape.

Our pliancy has enabled us to survive. We are physically
weak compared with many creatures, and have less acute
senses than some. Our rivals in the animal kingdom have
evolved faculties that we humans can only admire. But
other creatures have very little capacity to vary their way
of living. Indeed, on the lower levels, organisms follow
"fixed action patterns" from which they cannot depart, even
if the cost is life itself. Utilizing our incredible pliancy,
human beings have made the necessary adaptations at every
stage. We have survived generations of life in underground
caves; we have lived passively when necessary and become
pugnacious and territorial when such qualities seemed necessary for survival.

We too were wandering creatures, like the ape. We
shifted from the nomadic life to that of being mainly creatures of one place when we learned to harvest crops. Our
pliancy served us well. Remaining in one place soon felt
natural and seemed the right thing to do. The new life,
with the men off hunting and the women remaining at
home, came to feel natural before long. Virtually no other
creature could achieve such a psychological transition. In
addition to it, however, we introduced sharp sex differences,
which also came to feel natural. The extended notion of
property applied to women just as to land. Such changes
had consequences that affected us profoundly, and of which
we were unaware.

The child, in adapting to conditions in the home, calls
upon this same pliancy. For instance, the child becomes

competitive in a home where the parents respect nothing else. The adult's personality is the result of a sequence of such adaptations, though it does not feel like the result of adaptation at all. Paradoxically, this pliancy accounts for both our similarity when as members of the same society we adopt almost identical customs, and our diversity when as members of different societies we evolve different styles of life. Because of our adaptability, we absorb our accomplishments and our crimes; before long, they feel natural to us, and it becomes hard to picture ourselves as having acted otherwise, or being any different from the way we are.

The variety of adaptations a human can make is terrifying. Dostoievsky's quote, from which the title of this book is taken, goes this way:

> Man is a pliant animal—a being who gets accustomed to anything.
>
> *Prison Life in Siberia,* 1861

Accustomed to being a neurotic. A murderer. Accustomed to high achievement. To effortless independence. To new states of mental health that seemed utterly out of range for us. Accustomed to anything!

What's frightening is also what's most reassuring about this. The traditional psychoanalytic idea that basic character is already formed by age six offered a firmer sense of stability. One can't depart too far in a good direction or a bad one; changes occurring in our attitudes were thought to bespeak deep characterological conditions that existed all along. However, pliancy promises the continued possibility of novelty. Every outlook, desirable or undesirable, remains possible for anyone, no matter what his present outlook is. There are two distinct ways of viewing pliancy. From one point of view, environment shapes people's minds. Different influences and stresses might make members of the same society, even of the same family, quite different. *The alternative point of view is to think of pliancy as a faculty a person possesses.* It is the ability to assimilate any of an immense variety of visions of existence, and to feel that they are appropriate, indeed are the only ones reasonable for us to hold.

At present, the environmental view provides the foundation for almost every field of thought. It accords with the philosophy of science—more particularly, of the "hard sciences," such as physics and chemistry, which were designed to study inanimate matter. The great success of the environmental method with them seemed to commend it for use elsewhere. The environmental view is the dominant hypothesis of modern learning. Whether it is history, biography, sociology, or psychology, the influence of others—of environment generally—is studied in its various forms.

Schools of psychology differ in their evaluation of particular influences. All, however, view the person as essentially the result of outside influences of one kind or another. The topic of study might be the influence of parental treatment or of different teaching methods, of films, social customs, of advertising campaigns, or of 10 years of dictatorship on the minds of a populace. But in each case they are studying the impact of outside influences. This purpose is also fundamental in standard psychological experimentation. Experiments are always designed to test the "input" of particular stimuli on the person who is the subject, never to examine the way the person influences himself, adapts. It's as if the only way to study the inner life were to imagine it as produced by the environment.

As we all know, people interact with their environment. Yet our systems of analysis credit environment with too much power while failing to study the adaptive capacity that *people* possess. Only an understanding of this capacity can show people how to influence their own outlook in a deliberate way.

This is the interpretation I want to pursue, that of pliancy as a striving, active process. It is a creative capacity that belongs to the individual, a resource that has been crucial to our survival. We retain this capacity throughout life. Being misdirected, many people worry about being brainwashed, as if environmental masters had power over our minds. However, because pliancy is really an inner, personal capability we ought to concern ourselves more about making compromises for the wrong reasons. Acts that do violence to our beliefs can produce the very changes in us that we feared would be inflicted by the outside world.

To think of a person as adopting an outlook that grows natural, using innate plasticity this way, might appear counter to the whole orientation of the twentieth century. Mass media promote a kind of sympathy for the individual based on the view of him as a victim of forces. As soon as we broach the subject of the individual's behavior, dare to think of it as in any way *causing* his adaptation, his difficulties, it's as if we were displacing blame from the environment to the person. One can, however, grant the relevance of environment while maintaining that the person assimilated it, created his outlook by choices, by controllable acts that he need not have carried out. Suppose, for instance, the person could not possibly have anticipated the consequences, or weighed them, didn't appreciate alternatives that were there all the while. To simply wave over at environment and blame it for harm, without studying the person's own role in the outcome, is to defend the person from censure but at the cost of obscuring his real potential.

This is a mistake even when thinking about young children. We ask immediately how parents treated a child who is neurotic. But what about the child's treatment of his parents and others as a cause of his neurosis? If, for instance, lying is bad for the child, adds to his alienation and suspiciousness, and makes intimacy and true comfort impossible for him, we ought to know this fact. It would not be unsympathetic to note that the child has it within his power not to lie, since the child is really the one with the power to create a different outlook on life. Indeed, most psychologists would privately maintain this: that the child uses a real option in lying, and that lying is bad for him. It is a fault of modern psychological theory that it is equipped only to analyze *why* the child lies, to reveal pressures on the child toward lying that are different from those on his older and younger siblings who do not lie. The inquiry is important, but it has become a complete substitute for the study of how their own behavior affects people.

The seeming naturalness of whatever we've adapted to is essential to our pliancy. Actually, numerous decisions are involved in any adaptation—to one's home or to a larger society. A freedom was felt at certain moments, voids were filled in with decisions. But the nature of those decisions, even the fact that they were made, seems diminished in retrospect. We have the experience not of having adapted but of having *discovered* who we really are—as if the truth simply emerged. The illusion is complete. Although we have each produced our own adaptation, there is little or no sense afterward of our having made a series of uncertain assumptions. Our point of view, our whole way of thinking, would not serve us if we continued to experience it as only one of many. It needs a sense of rightness for us to feel safe in relying on it.

This same pliancy accounts for a host of difficulties into which we can fall, individually and collectively. Whatever adjustments we make tend to feel natural, including those with harmful costs. In such cases, the very ease of adaptation becomes the primary problem.

It seems an irony that what is most precious to us, our own personality and outlook, is constructed as an *unconsidered* by-product of choices we make. And yet I think this book will demonstrate that this is so. With an understanding of *why* choices leave particular traces, a great many things can be done. What seems natural to us—including fears, judgments, ways of perceiving that seem fully justified—has been arrived at by controllable behavior. By implication, it remains subject to change, and any sense of its being our inherent nature is merely an obstacle that must be taken into consideration when we attempt to change.

The study of pliancy aims at understanding *how choices affect the mind*. With such an understanding—for instance, of when choices leave harmful traces—we can make decisions deliberately to produce qualities in ourselves or erase them. We can revise our own psyches, and we can help other people find the choices that are best for them. Of course, I do not mean to imply that people will automatically drop all other concerns to reshape their outlooks. But producing such changes becomes feasible. The understanding of how our choices leave their traces seems precisely what is needed and could be enormously helpful in many ways. Indeed, the more comprehensive this understanding, the better our ability for deliberate personality change.

How are we to proceed, to learn enough about the pliancy we already possess for us to harness its power?

In the first section of this book, we shall see how the study of pliancy lost favor in psychology. Just why did psychology abandon this study? The second section is to be an analysis of pliancy, of exactly *how* people adapt. The implications are vast. The third section will examine some of these implications—for instance, those for self-help, for child rearing, for psychotherapy, for helping a friend with a problem, and for psychology itself as a profession.

CHAPTER TWO

Frontier Psychology

The idea that a person can exercise deliberate control over his outlook goes back many centuries. Whether it was Cicero telling us how to enjoy old age or Montaigne teaching us how to adjust to country life, the very giving of such advice presupposes some capacity on our part to make use of it. We would in some measure choose our adaptation to life.

Psychology as a profession began with this view of individuals as capable of making real choices. Its aim was to provide a body of knowledge with which we could enrich our lives. Its highest purpose was to lay bare our capacity for change, to show us how to become the people we wanted to be.

There was, therefore, every reason to believe that early psychology would investigate pliancy, in much the way I described it. As the study of how people regulate their inner destiny, psychology delved into how much control they really have over it and regularly investigated the effects on people of different behaviors.

Over time, however, it completely lost its bearings, abandoning its original purpose little by little and eventually disqualifying itself from such an inquiry altogether. It has developed not as a system to help people recognize their freedom and capacity for change, but as one theorizing that people have no such capacity. Every psychologist, or nearly every one, privately believes that people make real choices and can change themselves. But psychology, as a discipline, in none of its branches systematically studies exactly how much power people have and how their use of it affects them.

To see how psychology changed, it is useful to look at a set of basic beliefs that once guided its course and that it later surrendered. At the start, a set of assumptions was made and taken for granted. Although they furnished the whole direction for psychology and defined its inquiry, they themselves were not identified as important. That was understandable, since until we have an alternative we don't truly see the nature of a thing.

Early psychology rested on five assumptions. The *first* is that people's consciousness is real and should be studied. Inner experience, even if one's mental life can't be seen by another and in this sense verified, really does exist. The *second* is that people, using their minds, can discover their problems and what is needed for change. The *third* is that people make real choices and are not simply respondents to environment—that is, the individual truly initiates acts. The *fourth* is that people's choices affect their outlook. The *fifth* is that by a sequence of controllable acts, by an accumulation of the right ones, a person can produce real change in his mental state.

Interest in mind and belief in the power of will tend to go together. One must believe in mind, and in the independence of mind, in order to believe that people really make choices.

In the beginning, psychologists had no trouble accepting the notion of mind as real or of choices as real. When the earliest psychological laboratory was set up, by Wilhelm Wundt in 1878, its express purpose was to study the mind.

Wundt's primary aim, and that of his followers, was to resolve conscious experience into its elements. At the heart of their work was the study of feelings, sensation, and memory. Their aim was to improve people's mastery over these processes by learning about them. What was inside the mind could not be measured directly, but this in no way cast doubt on the belief that mind existed. Psychology was seen as the study of mind, carried on with the hope of enabling people to take steps to improve their own psyches when enough learning would be accumulated.

One form of psychology was uniquely American. It drew its point of view from American frontier thinking, which it took for granted. It never reflected upon the traditional beliefs. Unlike the typically introspective European psychology, its orientation was that of action and the freedom of the individual.

Frontier thinking had put its stock in freedom and independence. It valued courage and industry sanctified by deep religious conviction. The frontier was something not to limit one, but to be pushed back, and one could feel vibrance and the expectation of great adventure. There was a spirit of optimism in spite of hardships. Self-reliance was a necessity and not a choice. There were no parents or therapists stationed in the frontier towns to receive complaints from those who had made the hazardous voyage westward. Imbued with this spirit of self-reliance, the nineteenth century American outlook was full of hope. Freshness and morning were in the air. Speakers like Ralph Waldo Emerson exhorted audiences to assume responsibility for their lives and to rely on their inner strength. "A man should learn to detect and watch that gleam of light which flashes across his mind from within, more than the lustre of the firmament."

The incorporation of the frontier spirit into American psychology may be traced most directly through the influences on and writings of William James. James is one of the main characters in this story. Many in the field believe that modern psychology derives more from James than from Freud. Although himself from the East, James virtually personified frontier attitudes both in his own life and in the way he shaped psychology. He utterly reconstructed the psychology that had begun in Europe. For centuries conjectures had been made about how human beings received impressions and associate ideas. However, all such interest had remained a form of philosophy until the nineteenth century. James studied European psychology carefully and reproduced some of the basic research; during his later years as a professor at Harvard he gave his classes numerous experiments.

But James was more than a student of the mind. He imbued psychology with a pragmatism distinctly nineteenth-century American. With knowledge of the laws of consciousness, he believed, the individual can *change himself.* He can *do* something, and for James this meant he could do nearly anything. James made a number of assumptions and set his sights on particular forms of accomplishment. His "frontier" attitudes provided early psychology with a belief in the individual, with a commitment to the notion of freedom, and with dauntless optimism concerning people's capacity to overcome their problems.

James's grandfather, also named William James, had participated in the opening of the Erie Canal and the westward development along the Mohawk Valley. He had accumulated one of the great fortunes of the day. But the elder James's son, having little interest in money, had used the fortune to cultivate his tastes in people and in the arts. It was as if he had begun displacement of rugged individualism, which had earned the family fortune, to the challenges of examining the mind and its potential.

An occasional visitor to the home was Emerson himself. Indeed, after Emerson's very first visit he wrote that he had just seen "the lately born babe who was to become the second American William James." Henry, the second son, whose fame as a novelist was to match William's as a psychologist, wrote of Emerson, "I knew he was great, greater than any of our friends." Thoreau was also an early figure in the life of young William, along with many others whose very being became identified with spiritual faith and with belief in what Emerson called "the voices that we hear in solitude."

James's father needed no instigation to shun materialism. Young Henry was to write, "The rupture with my grandfather's tradition was complete; we were never in a single case, I think, for two generations guilty of a stroke of business."

Like his father's, William's exterior gave a sense of calm, and one could hardly guess the tragedies that all the members of the family fought against constantly, and not always successfully. They glided through life like swans, graceful, poised, but with legs churning desperately below the surface, unseen. The father had lost a limb through amputation. Both brothers suffered ill health and their sister Alice had to be looked after for melancholia. Perhaps because he had so much reason for despair, because the abyss was beckoning and near, William remained an active man, defiantly optimistic. Because of this unwavering optimism, many people came to regard him as their supreme hope. All his life he had a genius for friendship, making and keeping friends of very different kinds.

His illustrious career went from medicine to philosophy to psychology and then on to metaphysics. Like the successive removal of outer layers in his pursuit of the soul. He easily carried previous learning with him, and was a miracle of readiness to apply whatever he knew. He brought his medical knowledge about the brain and his pragmatism into psychology.

James remains unsurpassed in his ability to represent in words what conscious experience is like. From him comes the notion of consciousness as flowing "like a river or a stream." He leaves no doubt that psychology ought to center in the study of consciousness.

There is a stream, a succession of states, or waves, or fields (or of whatever you please to call them), of knowledge, of feeling, of desire, of deliberation, etc., that constantly pass and repass, and that constitute our inner life. The existence of this stream is the primal fact, the nature and origin of it from the essential problems, of our science.[35]

Unlike most of his predecessors in the study of consciousness, however, James was not content to watch it idly. Wundt had studied it like an astronomer. James emphasized the dependence of consciousness on will and was always mindful of the power of will to affect consciousness, indirectly if not directly. He could articulate the conscious experience of using the will as no one ever had previously or has since.

Suppose we try to recall a forgotten name. The state of our consciousness is peculiar. There is a gap therein; but no mere gap. It is a gap that is intensely active. A sort of wraith of the name is in it, beckoning us in a given direction, making us at moments tingle with the sense of our closeness, and then letting us sink back without the longed-for term.[34]

Frontier thinking never doubted human freedom or its importance, but James as philosopher recognized that freedom was not something anyone could prove. He wrote that "facts practically have hardly anything to do with making us either determinists or indeterminists. Sure enough, we make a flourish of quoting facts this way or that. . . . But who does not see the wretched insufficiency of this so-called objective testimony on both sides?" [33]

For James, the great adventure, the beckoning sea with all its treasures, was not merely the study but the *use* of consciousness. This meant the use of free will by people to produce effects on themselves. The challenge was what we did not yet know; the purpose of psychology was to take it up.

That this profound belief in freedom is itself a matter of choice is dramatically evident in James's own life. Following a deep depression, James wrote in his notebook that yesterday had been the crisis of his life. "I will assume for the present—until next year—that free will is no illusion. My first act of free will shall be to believe in free will. . . . I will go a step further with my will, not only act with it, but believe as well; believe in my individuality and creative power."

James remained convinced that his decision had been a crucial one. Years later, in his talks to teachers, he reaffirmed that "the very first act of a will endowed with freedom should be to sustain belief in the freedom itself."

The reliance of free will on consciousness has been made emphatically clear by James and others. Volition presupposes consciousness. By a voluntary action we mean only those activities preceded by a consciously held goal or purpose. The mind must give approval. Belief in consciousness and the reliance on free will, which formed the basis of James's psychology, were effortlessly accepted by American psychology, as part of a commonly held tradition.

For James, as for mankind, believing in free will was like saying, "Let's try the only door that may be open. If all the doors are closed, if we are helpless, there is nothing we can do. But if not, there may be much to gain."

In those days, animal consciousness was assumed by analogy. Just as we unhesitatingly feel that a pet dog or cat or canary is capable of thinking, so did the early psychologists. The animal was thought to be conscious when it exhibited the kind of behavior characteristically conscious in humans. Then, as now, people were prone to speculate about what went through the minds of animals. Poets had written man's passions into nature. Romantics had heard in the song of a nightingale or the neighing of a horse not merely a conscious response but seeming evidence of a transcendent consciousness. Shelley had beseeched the skylark, "Teach us sprite or bird/What sweet thoughts are thine."

Reaction to anthropomorphic thinking came first in literature. The essayist John Ruskin criticized such attributions as "the pathetic fallacy." Psychology likewise was soon to clamp down, first on anthropomorphism and then on any assumptions made about animal consciousness. But in James's day, whether animals were capable of consciousness and whether such consciousness, if it existed, resembled ours, were considered academic issues. Not until the start of this century did animal research become of real interest to psychology.

Nor was the problem of explaining consciousness in terms of brain physiology of any real import. The reductionist idea, best stated by a neurophysiologist recently, was that "all the phenomena of life would ultimately be reducible to the laws of physics and chemistry." [16] Whether or not enough might eventually be learned to do this was a question pondered at times by nineteenth-century writers. But the answer seemed so remote (practically nothing was known about brain physiology) that the reductionist proposition had no influence on early psychological thinking.

Psychology thus rested fully on assumptions made about human beings that could not be made about lower organisms. Not just the reality of consciousness and freedom of choice were assumed, but also the sufficiency of the human mind to comprehend what it needs to know and the capacity of the person to make the choices that would produce the desired change. These might be called the axioms of individual sufficiency. Psychology, it was thought, would help uncover the necessary insights and principles so that people could see what they needed and apply the discoveries to their own cases.

Because American psychology was to be used by people to change themselves, it was important to distinguish the voluntary from the involuntary. For James and G. Stanley Hall, and other American psychologists, change would occur within people as they regulated their decisions. Only in this way could they indirectly regulate feeling, which was not under the direct control of the will. Moreover, our actions influenced us *unfailingly.* James talked about the drunk who wouldn't want his last drinking spree counted against him. He may not count it, wrote James, "but his nerve cells and fibers are counting it, registering and storing it up." These early psychologists in the main took for granted the necessity of our being influenced by our own actions but did not make that assumption explicit.

American frontier enthusiasm thus applied to the single human being and was formalized in James's articulate psychology, which was studied by students everywhere in the United States and in Europe. A friend of James's, an idiosyncratic genius whom he brought to Harvard, named Charles Peirce, had made a startling assertion. Peirce said that every personal conviction we hold is a more or less sure indication of our having some habit or habits that caused us to hold that conviction. By this reasoning, dislike of ourselves must result from behavior of our own, as would a tendency to like ourselves. The idea seemed purely philosophical and was of no interest to psychology at the time. Perhaps it seemed too groundless to qualify as important. But James weighed it heavily in his thinking. It would take repeated actions of the same kind to change our way of thinking, James believed. He regarded our brain matter as "plastic." It holds its form; if it didn't, our personalities and outlook would undergo constant change. In other words, James believed, our actions exert a cumulative effect on our outlook, and to improve we must act in such a way as to produce the outlook we want.

Just as in frontier days, self-reliance combined with a belief in God, who would reward people for doing the right thing. Popular speakers of the day counseled their listeners not to worry about their feelings but to act properly. It is your purpose God looks at, and He will reward you. Early psychologists were affected by this kind of thinking. Although they did not put God directly in their formula, they counseled acting to "accumulate ethical forces." James himself was fond of using this term and often talked of "moral will multiplying its strength" when we make the right choices.

The idea that people can discover their "hidden powers" and utilize them was so thoroughly identified with the five axioms that, if any one of them were altered, the whole system would become powerless to achieve its purpose. They were its vital organs. Their necessity may be seen this way: Unless people are conscious and capable of choice (the first and third axioms), they are impotent to use psychology. Unless their actions do affect their subsequent mental states, there is nothing they can do (the fourth). The second and last axioms are *sufficiency* assumptions. The second asserts that one's mind can gather sufficient material to solve personal problems by taking proper action. It does not rule out self-deception or willful distortion but says that the mind is sufficient—even to puzzle out the devices that it sometimes employs against its own best interests. The last axiom asserts not only that we affect our minds, but that by the right strategies we can produce personality changes and keep them. It says that the power to produce the changes we want is in our hands.

The five axioms were indispensable in orienting psychology in its search for knowledge people could use to alter their mental states. The axioms did so by assuming that the critical knowledge existed and could be found. But if actions affect the mind of the person who engages in them, *how is one to know which actions will produce a desired effect?* Confronting psychology was the task of discovering principles that people could use to arrive at the decisions best for them. With such principles, people would weigh decisions and could act in ways that would profit them.

The axioms shaped every part of psychology. If people could possibly rely on themselves, if they had enough force to produce lasting changes, the axioms were necessary for finding the way. They were the quintessence of the system.

Then something remarkable happened.

Although psychology rested on these axioms, they had not been spelled out. No one had challenged them seriously as yet or proposed alternatives. Psychology was inchoate, as if still in bas-relief emerging from the wall of philosophy. Its necessary contours were not clear. Psychology needed these axioms but didn't know it. When any kind of difficulty was met, there was too great a readiness to surrender them and the challenge they presented. Gradually, without their having been specified, they were given up, and the field changed its direction utterly.

James's approach had definite flaws in it. Although it had seemed like common sense, it simply didn't work for many people. Not realizing its debt to the five axioms, psychology became willing to sacrifice first one and then others. As it did so, its whole form changed. It gave up its original purpose, surrendering both its optimism about the human capacity and its potential for discovering how far that capacity goes.

James's recommendation proved unusable for many people —and for most whose problems were of any complexity. It boiled down to a mere recommendation to act like the person you want to become. "We need only in cold blood act as if the thing were real, and it will infallibly end by growing into such a connection with our life that it will become real."

James suggested, for example, that "in order to feel kindly toward a person to whom we have been inimical, the only way is more or less deliberately to smile, to make sympathetic inquiries, and to force ourselves to say genial things." [35]

The recommendation just doesn't work. You can't create a feeling by pretending you already have it. People often discover when they try this method that their problems nag them as before but in addition they now feel fradulent. For many people, and for all of us at some times, the mere advice to act like the person you want to be is simplistic. The same actions will have different effects on the mind of the same person at different times. James had begun with the simplest form of self-help advice, and it didn't always work because people are too complicated.

What James did not realize is that certain knowledge of

one's inner state is necessary for calculating how to change it. People's solutions differ depending upon their condition. It is one thing to say that people have the power to change their mental states, another to say that merely imitating their ideals will do the trick. As it turns out, sometimes it will, but often it won't.

James advised us, in true frontier tradition, to pay minimum attention to our inner states. He bade us to "pay primary attention to what we do and express, and not to care too much for what we feel." He reasoned that since we cannot regulate our inner states by acts of will and can regulate them only by voluntary action, we should give full attention to the latter. But unless you study your inner state and know at least something about *yourself*, you won't know which actions to take.

American psychology overemphasized *action*. The real influences on the mind are *choices,* sometimes overt, observable choices, but also often choices that go unseen. The choice *not* to say something can exert as much impact on the mind as the choice to say something. James's psychology had regarded such "silent choices" merely as defaults that harm us or as failures to seize opportunities. However, the system that psychology originally sought could not be adequate without a full appreciation of the importance of such covert choices.

There is a real connection between underestimating the significance of feelings and overemphasizing the importance of actions. Often the choice *not* to act is a decision that results in greatly increased emotion. Many people act to discharge feelings that they would do better to experience and study so that other kinds of decisions can be made. Even a sense of helplessness, if one possesses it, is necessary to know about for one's own sake. A lifetime of activity, motivated by the desire to bury such feelings, proves hollow and unsuccessful, although the record of such a life may look good on paper. In fact, often the first step toward real and systematic change ought to be non-action for the sake of self-scrutiny, so as to magnify and bring to consciousness one's true state.

If James had a major flaw that was incorporated into his psychology, it was an almost pathological inability to acknowledge helplessness and real despair. He gave short shrift to such expression in others. Believing in a desired state of existence seemed necessary to make it true. He himself had contemplated suicide and afterward saw his vow to banish pessimism as vital. When others described their despair to him, and they often did, he would immediately respond that things were better than they seemed. He was so full of sympathy for all people, the tragedies that befell those around him pained him so deeply, that in a sense he denied the existence of tragedy. He fled from it by giving people advice, by exhorting them not to be overcome by it, and by conjuring up in their minds the picture of a brighter future, if only they would act in new ways. *Anything*, not to dwell on despair or look at it in detail. Perhaps fear of the kind of paralysis he had suffered when in despair remained in his mind. In his flight from pessimism, James did not amply appreciate how difficult it is to change or how strongly the past can seem to claim the future.

Most people with personality problems have at some time tried what James recommended, whether or not they have been influenced by his work. They have struggled to act in healthier ways. They found either that the system did not change them or that they could not even sustain the struggle. In his day, those failing to overcome their problems had no recourse. James's system seemed complete. One was left to conclude only that one had not tried hard enough. The system maintained that real, ultimate failure was impossible. It was even wrong to dwell on the thought of failure—and yet we all do. The system left people feeling responsible for their failures, and helplessly angry; it offered them no recourse.

American psychology had underestimated the severity of

human problems. The optimism that asserts all will be well began to look more like loyalty to a theory than to individuals, whose needs must be understood individually. Such optimism becomes an annoyance after a while. Frontier psychology began to look defective and, most damning, superficial. It seemed evident that real knowledge would not be so optimistic. "Optimism cuts a sorry figure in this theatre of sin, suffering and death," Schopenhauer had written, and this ironic insight certainly applied.

That psychology had thus far fallen short in its endeavor was beyond question. But the discipline was young, barely born in fact. There was no reason to conclude that it could not mature. The failure of this first attempt did not imply that psychology had attempted the impossible. There remained vast possibilities for studying how people could control their mental states. It was up to psychology to gather the necessary information and show them how.

Some brand new solution seemed called for—hope from a new source. A psychology was needed that would account for our feeling of helplessness and would talk about our history. It would explain our sense of a lack of freedom. It would treat us more gingerly. It would somehow accept our weakness while still holding forth promise that things could be different.

One might imagine that psychologists would study the work done by James to see how and why it failed. They never did, however. Psychology left its original track entirely, bypassing the work of James; it stopped investigating the individual's potential to change his own mental state, as if it had been proved that this was impossible. It no longer endeavored to give people insights they could use to change their lives. Instead, it embraced a whole new purpose.

CHAPTER THREE

Psychoanalysis: Gain and Loss

In Europe, the eighteenth century had exalted the power of the intellect. It had placed enormous confidence in the ability of reason to find answers. The accomplishments of Galileo and Newton and others seemed to argue that all things followed natural laws, which observation could reveal. There was belief in the comprehensibility of nature through the mind, through the use of dispassionate logic. But the Age of Reason had ended in great disappointment; in bloodshed, with the French Revolution and the others it inspired. Reason had caught passion aflame, and in the following years civil strife and angry mobs became a familiar sight in many parts of Europe. One wave of destruction followed another, as if mocking the optimism held by the previous generation. There seemed good reason to doubt that human beings were really free or that their rationality could ever prevail.

There was nothing new in the idea of human helplessness, in the notion that blind instincts govern our behavior. It had, however, been a philosophic notion. Now it was being elaborated upon in detail not just in the words of philosophers, but also in works of fiction, on the stage, and later in psychology. Schopenhauer wrote that what is conscious is only a small part of what takes place in the mind. There is a blind will with its own logic stronger than any we can put into action. The will is animal, Nietzsche agreed.

The idea that the unconscious is bad and that there is an impelling force springing from our animal nature, became an important issue in the Academies. Even those not at all pessimistic in their conclusions about the future of humanity believed in these unconscious forces and their enormous influence. Goethe saw in his "elective affinities" a force that draws people together, determining their lives, but not necessarily for the worse. And Dostoievsky, whom Freud greatly admired, was not a pessimist despite his recognition of the powerful unconscious urges and impulses that make us what we are. But it was essentially the ideas and philosophy of Schopenhauer and Nietzsche, concerning the passions and their implications, that Freud took for his own.

Darwinism had brought renewed respect for our animal nature. Our biology determines us more than we think. As Freud the medical student found himself drawn increasingly toward psychology, he believed he saw a way to keep his study of the mind consistent with biology. He would base his system of motivations on biological drives, on what he considered to be the instincts.

Freud's tremendous influence is attributable above all to the accuracy of his many perceptions of human behavior, and to his remarkable ability to identify what he saw. He was the first psychologist to observe whole regions of behavior and comment on them. In looking at the mind, its ratiocinations, he had Dostoievskian energy, and no psychologist could equal him. Moreover, he was tirelessly able to integrate what he saw into the system he constructed. Right or wrong, his interpretations stand as part of a highly complex scheme. Reading his work, one has the impression of being a visitor to a new planet. There are so many rules and interrelationships among the elements that one feels almost overwhelmed, if not unqualified to take issue.

Freud was without question the mapmaker of modern psychology. He was daring and comprehensive. Yet, for all his descriptive genius, the conclusions he drew are open to question. One difficulty is that it is hard to accept his observations, to give him the great appreciation he deserves, without also adopting at least the spirit of his explanatory system, which is highly deterministic. So seminal was Freud's work that it is sometimes difficult even to talk about minutiae of behavior that he observed without using his language, in which his deeply fatalistic assumptions are embedded.

Freud's theory of psychoanalysis rejected the idea that a person with a long-standing problem could on his own do anything to correct it. Rather, the theory assumed that people did not change because they were powerless to change themselves, despite any willingness on their part or knowledge that might be given to them. One reason Freud gave is that what he called the "libido," a general psychic energy that is sexual in its nature, becomes damned up, partially or almost entirely, in us. Although it manifests itself in different ways as we develop, it is not within our power to liberate our own libido in any appreciable way.

Freud left no doubt that there was need for an outside agent—a psychoanalyst.

> Our plan of cure is based on these discoveries. The ego is weakened by internal conflict and we must go to its aid. The position is like that in a civil war which has to be decided by the assistance of an ally from outside.[25]

Freud accounted for human helplessness by asserting that our character structure is formed by age six. By then, it has congealed but it remains active in governing us for the rest of our lives. This inner mechanism, which we ourselves cannot change, dictates our feelings and determines our actions in later life. No longer free, as in James's view, we must respond to commands from within. The mechanism inside us guides us over a trajectory that has been set early in our lives.

Freud considered *repression* the chief determinant of character structure. In childhood we bury key ideas, memories and feelings—repress them—because they are too painful for us to bear. As a result, the libidinal energy attached to them becomes lost to us. This repressed material, Freud believed, remains in the unconscious region, from which it influences our entire psychological life as an adult. Only by being repressed because of its unacceptability does an idea enter what Freud called "the unconscious." This meant that the unconscious is composed entirely of distasteful thoughts, feelings, and wishes. We are each a cauldron of hideous drives and ideas that we dare not allow ourselves to look at. Freud told us that it is largely because of repression that our hope for cure must rest with a psychoanalyst. Because of it, we cannot get in touch with our real underlying state and cannot learn enough about ourselves to cure a neurotic condition. This made psychoanalysis a necessity for anyone who wants real personality change.

At first Freud thought that the pleasure principle (the desire to seek pleasure and avoid pain) governed all unconscious mental life. Later he observed that people repeat acts, begun in childhood, that do not give them pleasure. He postulated the existence of a phenomenon that he called "repetition compulsion."

Although Freud constantly altered his theory in its details, he never changed its essential form. After a time he revised his ideas about sexuality and changed his beliefs concerning which were the dominant instincts in life. However, throughout his long and prolific career, he maintained his belief that character is formed in childhood.

Freud certainly did not disdain us for being helpless. On the contrary, he offered the consolation that we were heroic victims chained and bound, and many of us had long felt as if this were true. It was heartening to be likened to Greek heroes, like Oedipus and Elektra, who were themselves royal by nature but had been victimized. The attention given to our early lives ministered to a suppressed wish on the part of many people. We retain a yearning to assimilate better what happened to us as children, to clutch those early moments and to make more sense out of them than we did when we lived them. Others before Freud had argued the importance of childhood, and there were even theories of the unconscious. But Freud integrated these ideas into an elaborate system that purported to explain how character forms in childhood.

In effect, Freud told us that our failures to improve our own personalities, to overcome problems, had not been our fault. The problems lie too deep within for us to get at them. To offset this seeming knell of hopelessness was the great promise that Freud said lay in his new method of treatment. The psychoanalyst could do what we could not. He could "lift the veil of infantile amnesia" and "unmask the unconscious repressed roots of our problems." He could operate like a surgeon and free us, as Freud reported having done with patients in treatment. This new and wonderful psychology amounted to an offer of hope from a new source.

Psychoanalysis was thus a new way of thinking. It was for use by an expert who was treating not himself but someone else. It was not a furtherance of psychology as originally planned. It needed different pillars for support.

Of the early axioms, the only one fully satisfied by psychoanalysis was that consciousness is real. However, this consciousness fails to yield up to us sufficient information for diagnosis and cure. Too many of the crucial truths are lodged in the unconscious to permit that. Freedom and individual potential are seen largely as illusions, and psychoanalysis holds that even if we were free, our acts do not exert meaningful impact on our minds, so basic change in this way isn't feasible.

Freud became an extraordinary spokesman for the consistency of character. He had a rare talent for seeing similarities between different acts and between early childhood experiences and those much later on. He repeatedly pointed out that people who seemed on the surface to have changed were actually the same underneath. But in the process he stretched the case for consistency by assertions based on speculation. A little boy who was sadistic and became a murderer might be described as not having changed. But what about the same boy if he became a surgeon? Was he expressing the same infantile sadistic impulses, or had he truly gone on to adopt a new attitude toward his fellow man and to express it by saving lives? Freud could take acts that seemed to have nothing in common and argue that they were alternative forms of expressing the same impulses. The early sadism had been "sublimated." Doing surgery, by this reasoning, was merely an alternative expression of a sadistic impulse. The surgeon was thus not given due credit for his positive attitude toward humanity or a desire to help; he was conceived of as still like the murderer and as having changed only superficially. By such interpretations Freud made it seem that people change far less than they actually do.

Freud overlooked the possibility that even if we are the same over a period of time, such constancy may not indicate that we are victims of our personalities, but that by routine choices a person may unknowingly copy himself and thus remain the same.

Psychoanalysis regarded choices not as causes but merely as symptoms of a problem. The patient is in effect discouraged from dealing with these symptoms until their cause is found.

If someone had set out to contrive a system to discourage people from trying to help themselves, it might have made the very assumptions that psychoanalysis did.

From his earliest days, Freud pictured people as incapable of transcending their condition, and therefore as in need

of superior thinkers who could lead the way. These were
the great fathers of the world, those with unusual vision and
judgment. Freud's overwhelming desire to occupy the
father's role influenced all his relationships, just as it influenced psychoanalysis.

Freud believed from childhood that the world was waiting for him, as it had waited for Christ. In fact, even before
his birth, a prophecy had been made to his mother that her
son was to become a great genius and leader of men. By the
time Freud was 11, this prophecy had been strengthened by
others, and he believed them all. When he was 28, before
he had any idea how he was to earn his fame, Freud asserted
dogmatically that it would come. In a letter to his betrothed,
Martha Bernays, he wrote:

> I have just carried out one resolution which one group
> of people, as yet unborn and dated to misfortune, will feel
> acutely. Since you can't guess whom I mean I will tell you:
> they are my biographers. I have destroyed all my diaries
> of the past fourteen years. . . . Let the biographers chafe;
> we won't make it too easy for them. Let each one believe
> he is right in his conception of the development of the
> hero.[36]

In the Viennese Jewish society of Freud's day, the father
was distinctly the leader of the family. The father was never
wrong. In his absence the older brother was in command,
and others respected him as a father. Among the Jews, even
more than in most groups, older sons assumed responsibility
for younger ones. In fact, a fully adult son in trouble could
turn to an older brother for help and tradition required
the latter to take him into the business if possible. The
hierarchy was strict, and Freud believed in such a hierarchy. He always maintained one in his psychoanalytic
circle. Years later Freud's biographer, the psychoanalyst
Ernest Jones, was to write, "Of the five pre-war members it
was easy to say how Freud's affections were distributed.

Ferenczi came easily first, then Abraham, myself, Rank and Sachs, in that order."

With the image of Bismarck, the ideal of a father figure had been bright in the national mentality. Most people regarded their nation as the fatherland. Strong fathers were critical supports in the society. Teachers and, particularly, university professors were traditionally given a paternal role. They often advised students privately about their love affairs and upcoming marriages. Students would frequently stand in line to receive such personal advice.

Believing in the need for such a role and all it implied, Freud took enormous liberties with those in the private group that met weekly to discuss psychoanalysis and called themselves "the Committee." Though some were virtually his age and all were highly sophisticated, he treated them like young sons. For instance, he constantly made suggestions to the members regarding what to study, often letting them know he was disappointed in them. He told them where they ought to go to spread the ideas of psychoanalysis and held himself to be the arbiter of what they wrote, and even how they spent their time. For example, he warned Carl Jung not to spend too much time studying myths but to return to the study of topics Freud considered central to psychoanalysis. He was highly disagreeable when a member of his Committee did not immediately heed his advice and would frequently disparage the person in his absence.

Not surprisingly, Freud's fellow psychoanalysts broke with him altogether, one by one. Few remained at the end, and they were not the most prestigious. Even before he organized his Committee, Freud had run into trouble. Josef Breuer, a medical doctor with whom he had worked closely for more than a decade, left him abruptly. Freud wrote that Breuer "was the first to show that reaction of distaste and repudiation which was later to become so familiar to me, but which at that time I had not yet learnt to recognize as my inevitable fate." [23]

The first major defection from Freud's Committee was that of Jung. Then came Alfred Adler's. Freud demanded that Adler sever connections with his magazine as well as his organization. He wrote, "Enough that he is out of the society and that I am on good terms with Stekel, who has shown himself consistently loyal."

But not long after, Freud was to write, "I am so glad that now Stekel is going his own way. You cannot imagine how I have suffered from the labor of having to defend him against the whole world. He is an unbearable fellow." [36]

Freud suffered from a series of such disappointments and never seemed to understand their cause or to have any genuine interest in understanding them. Freud could never, not once in his life, say to one of his colleagues that perhaps he too had been wrong and seek reconciliation. It was not the father's role.

Freud's belief that people cannot make their way on their own, that they need a strong male leader, placed him in sharp contrast with incipient American psychology. Indeed, he himself recognized the egalitarian nature of American psychology and its belief in the individual. He constantly disparaged the United States and criticized Americans for the desire to exist as individuals without a dominant leader telling them what to do. He cautioned against the "psychological poverty of groups":

> This danger is most threatening where the bonds of society are chiefly constituted by the identification of its members with one another, while individuals of the leader type do not acquire the importance which should fall to them in the formation of such a group. The present cultural state of America would give us a good opportunity for studying the damage to civilization which is thus to be feared.[22]

According to Freud, the father is not someone who talks about his feelings, who explores his emotions or who admits his own irrationality. Although Freud made us aware of our emotional lives, there is always a sense that the deeper we get and the better we understand ourselves, the more ugliness we see.

The irony is that Freud himself was a loving person, a caring one, whose troubles with colleagues affected him deeply. Each time a break came, he felt it as the loss of a real friend, although he preferred to think of the rupture as the result of differences in theoretical viewpoints, or of the person's having an unresolved psychological problem. After a period of sadness he would pull himself up sharply. He had a policy of not allowing himself to dwell on past difficulties for long.

Adler's departure didn't bother him. But it broke his heart when Jung left. It wasn't just that Jung was conversant with an astounding range of myths and current literature, or that he was more worldly than the others. The two had dreamed together. Freud wanted Jung to go up the steps of immortality with him, perhaps even hand in hand. His own triumph would be less because Jung would not see him or love him.

That Freud was a deeply tender man and easily moved was evident in his letters, and in his expressions of devotion to whoever were his favorites at the time. But such feelings could cause him to stop, to savor experience, to rest from his purpose, which from early childhood had been unsurpassable intellectual accomplishment. He was a man at war with his own desire to be loved unconditionally and without words. It is easy to meet Freud with worship and to leave him in hate, as many of his contemporaries did. But this would not do justice to a man who was brimming with compassion and was controlled in the end by his own need for control.

His refusal to give due credit to emotionality and love in his own life is reflected in the superstructure of psychoanalysis. He saw people as driven by base motives, which they might at best refine and channel.

Built into all of psychoanalysis is a joylessness, a reductionism to the baser motives. Man is by nature not much good if you know what he amounts to, and life is not much fun. "Destructiveness is indestructible," wrote Freud in his essay on war. But what about the desire to see beautiful colors or smell fragrances or rub something soft? These may be as much a part of the human mammalian heritage as any of the instinct Freud mentions. We need something positive to build upon, not just the kinds of caveats that Freud found in his religious training and brought to psychology. Any sexual act whose aim was not procreation he condemned as a "perversion," the ultimate purpose of sex being to continue the species. But what about pleasures for their own sake, not just as preludes to coitus in order to multiply? Psychoanalysis left no room for unadulterated pleasure, only for purposeful pleasure. It was as if Freud, who felt hurried onward toward accomplishment from the time of his infancy, wished to impart that sense of urgency to us.

Freud glimpsed his own problem in moments, that his mind could never rest. He seemed incapable of passively experiencing joy of the senses but had to contain it, to analyze it, to master it by formulating the reasons for its existence. A passage in his essays "The Moses of Michelangelo" has always struck me as telling, but very sad. Freud wrote that when contemplating works of art, "I spend a long time before them, trying to apprehend them in my own way, i.e., to explain to myself what their effect is due to. Wherever I cannot do this, as for instance with music, I am almost incapable of obtaining any pleasure." [23]

This particular outlook has in the end cost psychoanalysis more adherents than any other—the pretense that we already know enough to explain all experience. It is a cover-up for fear of the unknown. If we claim to understand the unknown too quickly we will never learn about it. Nothing bad will happen if we stand before a work of art or put our arms around a loved one without fully understanding what the experience means. Psychoanalysis, if we take it too seriously, interferes with the flow of life. The patient is asked to understand the past before being free in the future; the student is asked to make judgments that reduce the force of the very things that move him most. It is well and good to seek understanding. But not everything is as yet reducible to a few instincts and a handful of primary processes, and there is no sense pretending that it is.

Freud's fear of the unknown, his inability to accept and enjoy the emotionality that he imperfectly understood, was a crucial determinant of his attitude toward women, for which he has often been attacked. He thought of women as distinctly inferior, once describing them as "the little creature[s] without a penis." The little girl's recognition that she has no penis, he theorized, was itself traumatic and left a permanent sense of inferiority upon her. As his many critics have pointed out, his underestimation of women's abilities went even beyond the prejudice against them characteristic of his time and place.

Freud's attitude toward women, like that of many men afraid of uncertainty and of their own emotions, was marked by exaggerated suspicion. Women are not just irrational but dangerously so, and loving a woman is perhaps the greatest pitfall in a man's life. For instance, Freud wrote:

> Women soon come into opposition to civilization and display their retarding influence—those very women who, in the beginning, laid the foundations of civilization by the claims of their love. . . . The work of civilization has become increasingly the work of men.[22]

Not in the early years, when he was writing love letters to Martha Bernays, but throughout much of his life, it seems that Freud would have preferred a world without women altogether. He certainly considered their demands for sexuality and love to be hazardous. Civilization, he believed, was based on the sublimation of sexual desire, the conversion of it into a higher form of energy, which could be used for creativity. Women opposed this and were always a threat to pull men down. In seeking sexual love, he wrote, a man "made himself dependent in a most dangerous way on a portion of the external world, namely, his chosen love-object, and exposed himself to extreme suffering if he should be rejected by that object or should lose it through unfaithfulness or death. For that reason the wise men of every age have warned us most emphatically against this way of life." [22]

The experiences of an individual would not ordinarily matter so much, but in Freud's case they are important. Seldom has anyone so imposed his own experiences on the thinking of a discipline as Freud did. In addition to his ideas, his attitudes and even his mood left their mark on psychoanalysis and influenced psychology generally. For instance, Freud himself apparently felt comfortable only in a certain kind of relationship, that in which he was the father giving advice to his sons. And he surmised that almost invariably the sons came to resent the father. It was partly on the basis of such observations that he postulated as a universal phenomenon the Oedipus complex, in which the son wants to make love to his mother and kill his father. He regarded the Oedipal wish as having a long history.

> We cannot get away from the assumption that man's sense of guilt springs from the Oedipus complex and was acquired at the killing of the father by the brothers banded together.[22]

The truth is that some fathers incur resentment and others do not. A child will have moments of resenting either or both parents. Had Freud been more open to examining relationships of other kinds, and to seeing their potentialities, he might not have announced that the Oedipus complex is a critical and universal phenomenon.

This was perhaps Freud's most serious mistake, certainly the one he has been criticized for most often, that of assuming that everything that happened to him was the lot of all mankind. He even imagined that his difficulties in getting along with people reflected a universal tendency, like that of growing older or the body's decay. Late in life he wrote: "Against the suffering which may come upon one from human relationships the readiest safeguard is voluntary isolation, keeping oneself aloof from other people." [22]

The reductionism of psychoanalysis, which had great influence on psychology generally, owes a good deal to conclusions Freud drew based on his interpretations of his own experiences. Psychoanalysis thus introduced into psychology a series of assumptions about people that no one fully responsible for his own life could afford to make.

Freud made it as hard as he could for anyone to overthrow his conclusions. He was quick to disqualify anyone who tried. When others who believed more strongly than he did in the individual's potentialities took a stand against psychoanalysis, he had a ready argument against their right to disagree with him. Of the patient in psychoanalysis who expressed skepticism, Freud said:

> One does not regard his attitude as the effect of his judgment at all, for he is not in a position to form a reliable judgment on the matter: his distrust is but a symptom like his other symptoms. [23]

Regarding the skeptic who is not a patient, Freud wrote:

> We have been obliged to recognize and express as our conviction, that no one has a right to join in a discussion of psychoanalysis who has not had particular experiences which can only be obtained by being analyzed oneself. [24]

Beyond being helpless, we are even helpless to understand why we are so helpless.

As part of the downgrading of the individual's potential came a new emphasis in psychology. Instead of helping people use their freedom to better their lives, the new emphasis was on predicting people's behavior. Early psychology did not concern itself with the issue of whether another person could predict what one was going to do. What I do is up to me. The important thing was to act in ways that would produce desired effects. But psychoanalysis took seriously the assumption that the human being is, in theory, prefectly predictable. Freud's own respect for human complexity prevented him from making many predictions about the future. However, he set for himself the task of understanding behavior as if it were always a predictable outgrowth of knowable facts. Someone's choice of profession, or an irrational fear, or even suicide, was theoretically predictable if only we knew enough about the person's early character formation.

Most important, Freud set a new task for psychology, that of accounting as fully as possible for behavior, of identifying its causes. This is a very different purpose from that of studying the efficacy of different kinds of behavior. Psychoanalysts who differed with Freud regarding the causes of behavior nonetheless adopted his purpose without considering it. They simply put forth different theories of causation. For instance, Freud has posited that the instincts of sex and self-preservation were crucial determinants of character and of adult behavior. Alfred Adler had his own theory, Otto Rank his, Sandor Ferenczi his, and so forth. However, all shared the purpose of finding the causes of behavior—of discovering why people act as they do. So did subsequent psychologists, including those who disparaged virtually everything Freudian. The question has considerable merit. But Freud had shifted the purpose of the field from showing people how to *use* their freedom to that of accounting for people's behavior as if they had no freedom at all.

Freud also applied his concept of theoretical predictability to characters who had lived in the past. Determinism is an easily made assumption about a life already lived and completed. There can be no refuting it. For instance, he related

Leonardo da Vinci's difficulties in finishing masterpieces to events in the artist's childhood that supposedly molded his character. It is easy to be deterministic about a life already completed. Other psychoanalysts wrote similar kinds of analyses of past lives.

All this amounted to a tremendous change in approach from the American psychology based on self-reliance that James had developed. The Freudian influence did more than substitute the idea of therapy for self-help. It introduced a particular kind of therapy reflective of Freud's own outlook on life.

A cornerstone of the psychoanalytic movement is the idea that until early causes are brought to light and reabsorbed by the patient, there can be no cure. There cannot be rebirth until the past has been understood and dealt with. Over the years psychoanalytic therapy has undergone many variations. But its implicit underestimation of the individual, and especially the notion that the therapist is responsible for the cure, remain. It is not enough for the modern therapist to say that the patient must produce his own cure. This is merely paying lip service to the individual's capacities. The system of psychoanalysis, and of psychology that evolved from it, is set up not directly for the individual's use but for the therapist to arrive first at the crucial insights and to accomplish the cure.

At first Freud thought that merely bringing the past to light would be enough to effect cure. He had been greatly influenced at the start of his career by certain of Breuer's discoveries. Breuer, who had been practicing right in Vienna, had used hypnosis in a novel way. Instead of the usual method of suggesting to patients under hypnosis that a symptom would disappear, Breuer did nothing more than talk to his patients about their symptoms. Sometimes this actually helped. Then one day a patient described to Breuer the onset in childhood of a particular symptom, and to the surprise of both, the symptom disappeared. Breuer later told Freud of this "miracle," after which the two commenced their collaboration. Together they sought to have patients under hypnosis work their way back to the rediscovery of significant episodes that produced their problems. Freud and Breuer believed that where there were symptoms, a "quantum of energy" had been "bound up" due to some early experience. The purpose of their method was to release that energy.

But some patients who made such discoveries underwent no change. Their symptoms hung on. Apparently, it was not enough to make the forgotten memory conscious. Something more was needed.

Working alone for a long period, Freud went on looking for the key to freeing the patient from his past. For a time he thought that it lay in his communicating back to the patient what the analyst had learned about the patient's past. It was important that the patient accept the truth emotionally and not merely disclose it. Freud had much earlier abandoned hypnosis in favor of his now famous technique of having the patient lie on a couch and report what passed through his mind. Freud was by now certain that neurosis was always caused in childhood and that the cause was sexual. And he remained as certain that cure required getting the patient to become conscious of forgotten memories. Only by recapturing childhood incidents and fantasies could the patient become free of the past that enslaved him. Being a victim of his past, the patient needed release, and Freud continued his search for the form that this release would have to take.

All along, Freud made the stunningly optimistic assumption that the patient's consciousness of those early events and what they meant would be curative. He had no doubt that the truth, if the patient could just feel it properly, perhaps experience it repeatedly, would set the patient free. W. H. Auden described this belief about cure in a verse about Freud:

> He merely told
> the unhappy Present to recite the Past
> like a poetry lesson till sooner
> or later it faltered at the line where
> long ago the accusations had begun.

However, nothing seemed enough. In some cases the patient could talk incessantly about early experiences, could feel them afresh and bemoan them, could explain how they might evoke expectations different from those reasonable in the present, could do all this—and yet remain unchanged.

As Freud gathered his Committee round him, he remained staunch in his beliefs about the importance of the past. He maintained that anyone who argued that we can cure a problem on our own, or without recourse to the past, was not a true psychoanalyst. Yet it grew increasingly evident that his method was not fulfilling the promises he had made for it. In the words of Clara Thompson, later a psychoanalyst of great repute, "By 1920 psychoanalysis as a method of therapy was at its lowest ebb. Enough years had gone by to show that psychoanalysis as it was practiced did not bring permanent cure." [55]

Freud himself recognized the failure of his method. However, he was prepared to explain that failure in only one way. Not only does character structure form in early childhood, he explained, it congeals into a state so solid that the tools of treatment can often do little to alter it. The patient is helpless. And so, in a great many cases, is the psychoanalyst.

Increasingly, Freud turned his interest away from therapy to the problem of understanding society. His theory that the mental mechanism becomes fixed and that people are too weak to change themselves on their own, even his theory that knowing the past is crucial for change—these ideas are not truly put to the test when one is talking about a whole society or speculating about the origins of civilization.

Freud himself came to despair of psychoanalysis as a treatment method, just at a time when his early hopeful writings were becoming widely accepted. In 1937, in an essay called "Analysis: Terminable and Interminable," he wrote:

> You are perhaps aware that I have never been a therapeutic enthusiast. . . . Every analyst ought periodically himself to enter analysis once more, at intervals of say five years, and without any feeling of shame in so doing. So not only the patient's analysis but that of the analyst himself has ceased to be a terminable and become an interminable task.[23]

How many people would enter analysis, or would believe in the method, if they knew that? In the same period Freud wrote:

> We must not be surprised if the difference between a person who has not and a person who has been analyzed is, after all, not so radical as we endeavor to make it and expect that it will be. . . . Sometimes the effect of analysis is simply to raise the power of the resistance put up by inhibitions, so that after analysis they are equal to a much heavier strain than before the analysis took place.[23]

Freud's promise of a therapy method had persuaded great numbers of people to give up belief in their own ability to cure themselves of problems. Now he was saying that after a lifetime of research, he virtually had no method.

His giving up on his method of cure meant nothing to those who had not believed in psychoanalysis in the first place. But to the millions of people who had come to believe that their childhood had doomed them, it was a sad note indeed. And psychology, which had begun to give up on the individual potential, never recovered. It never again devoted itself to enhancing people's ability to cure themselves of problems.

Psychoanalysts tried to make a variety of corrections of Freud's method, both during the latter part of Freud's life and after his death. But it was simply not within the province of psychoanalysis to think of the human being as continuously reconstructing his own psyche by choices. One could not be a psychoanalyst without believing in the idea that character structure is fixed in the past or without believing in "psychic determinism," the doctrine that our mental apparatus determines our choices. Freud's daughter Anna, also a psychoanalyst, noted this. She commented that whenever interest was transferred to the power of the ego, the part of the psyche that chooses and is conscious, "it was felt that here was the beginning of apostasy from psychoanalysis as a whole."

A profound sense of the individual's helplessness may be felt in the writings of even those psychoanalysts now regarded as radical. For instance, Harry Stack Sullivan, considered to have departed sharply from Freud's position, wrote:

> Our awareness of our performances, and our awareness of the performances of others are permanently restricted to a part of all that goes on and the structure and character of that part is determined by our early training; its limitation is maintained year after year by our experiencing anxiety whenever we tend to overstep the margin.

Sullivan was one of a group of psychoanalysts who stressed the importance of interpersonal relationships in affecting personality. Another of the neoanalysts, Karen Horney, was heavily criticized by colleagues for paying insufficient attention to childhood experiences. She saw people aggravating their problems by entering what she called "vicious cycles." For instance, an insecure child becomes a braggart; antagonizes people throughout adolescence; then, seeing people's adverse reactions, becomes more insecure; brags more; and so forth. Horney, along with a number of others, also took issue with Freud's particulars—his overlooking of the social forces affecting a person in adult life and his attitudes toward women. But because she was essentially a psychoanalyst, Horney was far from assuming the original five axioms and trying to build a system from them. For her, as for Freud, the trajectory of a psychic life was set.

The interpersonal psychoanalysts, who practiced in the United States and England, relied on the treatment method of giving the patient new reactions. They believed that, if shown warmth, the person would view himself more positively. The impact of harsh past evaluations might be overcome. But this method too misses the point. Warmth and sympathy help sometimes, but only temporarily. If favorable reactions to people could really cure them, most people would have changed before entering therapy. And there would be no need to pay high prices for so simple a remedy or to spend years training therapists in how to apply it. But love, praise, even good reactions from a prestigious person are far from enough.

Nor is the problem essentially interpersonal. If it were, a fresh start, say in a new town, would make a major difference, and we know it seldom does. People remain the same because they unknowingly create the same frame of mind, day after day—by the complex pattern of choices they undertake. And the psychoanalytic movement, despite its modifications of Freud's beliefs, does not address itself to studying the way people's choices affect them.

One can view much of latter-day psychoanalysis as an attempt to correct its original position. Psychoanalysis tried to come back to a point of view that assumed choices matter. But it couldn't. Its premises make such a position impossible. Analysts themselves often sense this and smuggle in particular techniques that are not dictated by their position. But they lack a systematic way of understanding how patients can really use their choices in their own behalf. They make spot recommendations but lack a basic theory and approach.

Today there are just about as many techniques as there are individual psychoanalysts. Some psychoanalysts, adhering strictly to Freud's system, avoid making suggestions or giving advice of any kind. Others give advice continually. Some believe in the instincts that Freud described. Others do not. Some believe, as Freud did, that all the material in the unconscious is potentially painful if discovered, that it was forced into the unconscious by repression. Others hold with

Jung that there is a higher nature in human beings, that the unconscious is full of potentially ennobling aspirations and memories. Some believe in the absolute dominance of the sexual urge. Others believe, as Adler did, that the primary urge is a struggle for power. Some avoid talking about the patient's transference and themselves remain anonymous as far as possible during treatment. Others insist that the patient discuss his feelings about them. They drag such feelings into consciousness and discuss and interpret them, making this a large part of their treatment method. Some make interpretations sparingly. Others try to dazzle patients with interpretations made even before the first session is over. Psychoanalysts differ in how they handle resistance, and even in what they consider to be resistance. And if you report the same dream to ten different analysts, you will very likely receive almost as many different interpretations of that dream. What psychoanalysts have in common is mainly the use of the same language and a commitment to psychic determinism.

The position taken by psychoanalysis on two issues is especially important in the light of events to come. These are animal research and, more generally, the scientific status of such work. Freud thought that certain of his findings might apply to animals other than human beings. This is not surprising since Freud was an ardent follower of Darwin. He wrote:

> This central schematic picture of a physical apparatus may be supposed to apply as well to the higher animals, which resemble man mentally. . . . Animal psychology has not yet taken in hand the interesting problem which is here presented.[25]

But at no time did it occur to Freud to carry out experiments with animals in order to learn about the human psyche. Relying as he did on a talking cure, he would hardly have tried such an approach. He was not one to wait for other disciplines, such as zoology or animal psychology, to catch up to him before going ahead in his own direction. He took the same attitude toward science generally. Freud did not doubt that reductionism of all psychological findings, including his own, to the laws of biology might be possible some day. But this would be a problem for others. Freud wrote that:

> We must bear in mind that some day all our provisional formulations in psychology will have to be based on an organic foundation. It will then probably be seen that it is special chemical substances and processes which achieve the effects of sexuality and the perpetuation of individual life in the life of the species.

Perhaps every bit of sound advice ever given by one person to another has an "organic foundation." But it would seem insane for people to stop talking to each other, to stop trying to help one another until everything they said could be backed by laboratory findings. To play it safe in this way would be to stop living. Ernest Jones put it: "Doubtless all psychologists expected, as they still must do, that one day scientific law and order would prevail in the apparent chaos of mental processes as it has in other sections of the universe."

But Jones, writing some years after Freud's death, concluded that, "Brain physiology has turned out to be even more refractory than psychology itself."

Psychoanalysis has given us innumerable observations of patterns of human thought and behavior. It seems inconceivable that other animals can come near matching human subtlety and complexity. And the more we learn about the intricacies of the human mind, the further behind laboratory science seems in its capacity to account for what we know. Freud's speculations on the hidden meanings of phenomena, though often far-fetched, shine a spotlight on personality brighter than any before him. Above all, Freud communicated his great excitement in studying the mind, his feeling that nothing is too small for scrutiny, that behind any act or even any fantasy may lie a grand history. As the greatest identifier of phenomena in the psychic world and supplier of a vocabulary, he is assured of continued fame. It is too bad that thus far a major effect of the knowledge he gave us has been to increase a sense of dependence and helplessness. But that was a necessary result of the assumptions Freud and his followers made about human beings.

It can certainly be no advance for psychology to disregard the world of observations that Freud and his disciples made. To this day he is the only psychologist whose system comes near doing justice to the complexity of personality. A half-century of dedication to the workings of the mind is mirrored in his more than 5,000 pages on the subject, ideas evolved from a remarkably consistent vantage point. Many of his conclusions are doubtless without warrant. He loved to believe in the unlikely. However, he had too many pene-trating insights for us to simply turn our backs on his work. The body of knowledge he gave us cannot be discounted. It is unfortunate that the starting place he chose was to assume human incapacity.

The ideal next step would have been to take what we learned from Freud and to reinterpret it where necessary. There was no necessity to reach such pessimistic conclusions. Psychology need not have abandoned its belief in the individual's capability.

Yet the next major development in psychology drew it even further from its original purpose.

CHAPTER FOUR

Behaviorists:
Specialists at Control

The time has come when psychology must discard all reference to consciousness. . . . Its sole task is the prediction and control of behavior, and introspection can form no part of its method.[60]

So wrote John Broadus Watson, the father of behaviorism, in 1914.

How can one possibly call himself a psychologist and not believe in a psyche? And why should anyone who can think deny the existence of people's consciousness, of their mental processes? It takes a mind confused by learning to deny the existence of the obvious. And yet a movement within psychology that denies the existence of mental events, and of freedom, has become enormously influential.

The roots of this idea too were in the Age of Enlightenment, which had done so much to advance science and free the modern mind of superstitious fear. It had set down the very principles of scientific methodology. Its great success

48

had invited the idea that the whole universe is a complex machine operating according to strict mathematical laws. Nothing is random or free. An objective approach could continue to teach us those laws, it was believed.

In the nineteenth century, science continued its conquests. The empirical approach, demanding strict verifiability so that experimenters could duplicate their findings, seemed to have made the difference between modern life and that of medieval man. It appeared only natural to try to extend the methods of science wherever they could possibly go, even beyond geology, biology, and chemistry. The idea evolved that even progress in understanding human nature would depend upon the strict application of scientific method to human problems.

In the middle of the century, Auguste Comte proposed a system of inquiry that would make the same demands of human experience that had been made when investigating other subject matter. That such a method had been developed for use in the observable, material world seemed unimportant. The criteria of science were considered inviolable. This necessitated an adjustment in Comte's approach. Though we could not be positive of another person's thoughts, we could study social interactions, which reflect those thoughts at least partially. Comte began the philosophic movement known as "positivism" and founded the field of sociology, a term he invented as well. He was perhaps also the first of a series of "non-psychologists"—those who took the trouble to define the inner life as nonexistent.

Toward the end of the nineteenth century, a movement began in Vienna, Freud's own city, called logical positivism. It asserted that a thing could have no meaning unless it could be empirically demonstrated. Whatever cannot be defined or verified does not exist. That proved satisfactory for much of physics, at least for a time, and it gave a seeming simplicity to thought. In view of the rapid progress of the natural sciences, it seemed to some only reasonable to consider a similar approach in psychology.

But the dilemma remained. There had, of course, been no progress in the effort to verify observations of psychic events. People's inner lives were as private and as unverifiable as they ever had been and doubtless would always be. There was the possibility, indeed the actuality, of events knowable to one person only. One person can't feel another's pain, and yet are we to say it is meaningless when a friend says he is in less pain than yesterday?

Psychology had a choice. It could relent on the criteria that applied in the mechanistic universe. Because people's inner lives cannot be seen or measured by others, it might have reasoned, these criteria are not appropriate—at least not in their usual form. The alternative was to insist on these criteria. Such was the position of the behaviorists.

Behaviorism originated largely as a way of counteracting the unreliable and speculative nature of psychology as it had existed. Too much of psychology consisted of merely stating some new theory about the mind. Though it seemed that considerable knowledge had been accumulated, there was a major problem in distinguishing the part that was real from that which was mere speculation. Behaviorism, by applying the standards of physics and other objective sciences to the inner workings of the mind, sprang out of an attempt to make such distinctions. Behaviorism began quite reasonably; however, it ended, ironically, with the refusal to deal with the very subject matter it sought to explain.

The great animal researcher Ivan Pavlov, whose research was the model for the behaviorists, had talked repeatedly about the mental state of his animals. Although he took objective measurements wherever possible, he could not sensibly avoid the realization that even lower animals might have inner lives. He referred to the "alertness" of his animals, to their "somnolence," to their "irritability," to their "states of awareness," and to their "distractibility." He even credited his dogs with a "freedom reflex," which appeared in animals that struggled to avoid being strapped in the experimental harness. Pavlov never took seriously for a moment the idea that a dog was merely an automaton—devoid of mind and volition.

Watson's original point of view was not that animals are without inner states; rather, he wanted to eliminate such subject matter from his research, since he could not apply the criteria of measurability to the inner lives of lower animals or of people. But gradually the decision not to study something, to treat it as if it was not there, led behaviorists to actually believe it did not exist. They lost sight of the fact that they were studying only the shadow of the subject matter that once had comprised psychology.

Watson's purpose was simply to see how useful a system he could develop using only those methods that had succeeded in the laboratory. In his volume *Behavior: An Introduction to Comparative Psychology*, he admitted that "feelings are one of two serious 'stumbling blocks' in the way of a strictly objective psychology." The other is thinking. "If the thought processes and affective states cannot be reduced to behaviorally observable phenomena, the whole behavioristic program is in grave danger of collapse."

Watson tried to avoid talking about unverifiables, such as people's thoughts, by concentrating on behavior, which could be observed by others and could be measured. For instance, a person reporting about his inner life was saying something, and his statements themselves could be measured. It seemed common sense to Watson that since we exist in the physical universe, all our mental processes must have physical existence and ultimately be measurable. Watson speculated, for example, that when people think, the larynx moves, as if all thinking were covert talking to oneself. One cannot see another's thoughts, but these supposed movements of the larynx could be recorded, measured, and treated scientifically. Watson's experiments failed. But the point is that he believed in mental processes and was simply trying to trace them through their counterparts in the physical universe.

As we have seen, both Freud and James believed that mental processes exist in the physical universe also. But what distinguished behaviorism was its decision not to deal with any process unless it could be recorded objectively and measured scientifically. Psychologists who were predecessors of the behaviorists felt it their domain to deal with unmeasurables, without holding themselves back until instrumentation and techniques for recording mental processes could be devised. The behaviorists refused to consider that the nature of psychology might be fundamentally different from that of physics, that different criteria of acceptance and of verifiability might be needed to help the field progress.

A related difficulty encountered by the behaviorists was that ordinary scientific methods are devised for beings who do not exercise choice. They are designed for studying a mechanistic universe. One can only apply formal scientific method if one assumes that the objects being studied are not capable of independent action. Therefore, Watson's decision for the sake of applying his method was to regard people's freedom of choice as outside his domain. This, too, was necessary for one in search of a truly objective method, one precisely the same as that used to study the physical universe.

Watson had done his Ph.D. thesis in 1903 using white rats as subjects. By the 1920s behaviorists had shown a marked preference for using animals in their research. Since mind was not being studied, the gap between rats and humans appeared diminished. The behaviorists' purpose was to discover laws of behavior that held for subhuman animals and then to apply those laws to humans. Working with animals offers several advantages. The behavior of lower animals is simpler to study and control. Rats behave more like one another than humans do. Their motivations are simpler. A hungry rat won't starve itself for an ideal or to prove a point. Besides, it is easier to control experimental conditions than when experimenting with human beings. Animals can be bred in captivity, their food cycles regulated over a lifetime, and their behavior observed. Nor do lower animals have recourse if they are starved or deprived of water for the sake of an experiment.

A huge oversimplification had begun. Having made the assumption that human beings are like rats but harder to study, the behaviorists limited themselves to examining characteristics possessed by both people and rats. They doomed themselves to overlook qualities of mind that human beings alone possess. Some cited Darwin's discovery that human beings are merely animals—a discovery that had opened the door to biological research on animals. But Darwin would never have drawn the same conclusions as the behaviorists. On the contrary, he was concerned with differences between species, and with the role that such differences play in fostering the survival of the species. Our special kind of intelligence, which has given us our incredible adaptability, has been crucial for survival. Studying humans as if we are merely more complicated than rats but not essentially different was a preposterous mistake. It amounted to a decision to bypass human psychology in order to study something much simpler, and very much less important.

Originally, Watson's plan was to see how far a discipline could be developed dealing wholly with what could be seen and measured. As late as 1953, behaviorists were cognizant of the existence of inner lives, but felt that, not being observable, they could not be studied. In that year B. F. Skinner, later to become the spokesman for the movement, wrote: "The objection to inner states is not that they do not exist, but that they are not relevant in a functional analysis." [50]

As they studied people's verbal reports, behaviorists recognized that these were reports of something that went on inside. A verbal report could be true or false, or, for instance, "reasonably accurate." They used the terms *reward* and *punishment*, which implied that even a lower animal felt satisfied in some sense or felt displeasure over what was done to it. Behaviorists, in other words, still asserted that a person, or even an animal, reacts to its own inner state, which in turn has been subject to influence by the way one has treated the person or animal.

Then modern behaviorism underwent a most remarkable

transition. Gradually, disregard of inner states became translated into absolute *denial of their existence*—at least in the writings of Skinner and his followers. Across the country it was no longer permissible for students of behaviorism to talk about the accuracy of verbal reports. That implied that they were reflections of something inside the organism. The words *reward* and *punishment* were likewise condemned as too subjective. The true behaviorist had a commitment never to be caught carelessly referring to an inner state. One had to think of animals and people as simply responding to what was done to them. In place of *reward,* behaviorists introduced the term *positive reinforcement.* If a procedure by an experimenter, such as giving the animal food, elicited more of some performance, then the act was a *positive reinforcement.* An act that curtailed behavior was likewise a *negative reinforcement.* The purpose became one of finding a language that did justice to the picture of living organisms as having no inner states. What had originally been a working hypothesis seemed to behaviorists now to be the only logical way of viewing people. Skinner, by then, regarded inner states as metaphysical, in the same category as religious notions:

> By arguing that the individual organism simply reacts to its environment, rather than to some inner experience of that environment, the bifurcation of nature into physical and psychic can be avoided.[49]

Yes, it can be avoided. But the question remains: Does a rat or a pigeon, or for that matter, a human being, really react to the environment or to *its experience* of that environment? To avoid a question is not tantamount to solving it.

Slowly behaviorists grew more confident that their way of picturing human beings was the only sensible one. Their work, often embellished by abstruse mathematics and the terminology of science, seemed appropriate for the university. There the battle between medical and nonmedical authorities over who is qualified to do therapy played an important role. Psychology had increasingly become the province of nonmedical authorities trained in the university. The new emphasis on being like other scientists helped give psychology departments a new status, and partly for this reason, they began to emphasize such subjects as physiology and higher mathematics. Behaviorism, having fashioned itself as scientific, began to push psychoanalysis and other forms of "nonscientific" psychology out of the universities. Behaviorists were not yet doing therapy themselves and many condemned those who did as too speculative. They demanded of those who would be therapists that they take advanced courses in statistics and in scientific method. Surely the ability to reason will prove important to being a good therapist, but proficiency in such subjects as statistics has yet to be demonstrated as relevant to understanding an individual or helping him. The criterion of being scientific, however, limited the number of practitioners in the field, and this was acceptable to medical doctors and to professional psychologists alike.

The real sufferer was the student whose interest in the psyche had attracted him to psychology in the first place. Even if his major was called clinical psychology, he was taught in many schools that therapy was unproven and was actually worthless. He learned little about mental processes and was forced to study material far from his interest. During the 1950s and early 1960s, behaviorists existed almost exclusively in universities. There they frequently decided upon the syllabus that students who wished to become therapists had to study.

With their increasing power, behaviorists not only set standards for would-be practitioners in many places, they also felt freer to make enormous claims. Along the way, they themselves became convinced of the truth of their early hypotheses—that mind and choice are nonexistent. And they began to teach these ideas as if they were proven facts, to hundreds of thousands of students. A definitive textbook used by undergraduate psychology students throughout the United States contained the following assertion:

> So long as life endures, a creature's behavior is a clay to be molded by circumstances, whimsical or planned. Acts added to it, and other acts which fall out, are the means by which it is shaped. Like the two hands of an artisan, busily dabbing and gouging, are the two processes, *reinforcement* and *extinction*.[38]

By *extinction*, behaviorists mean nonreinforcement of already learned acts.

Remarkably, Skinner himself forgot that his original non-acknowledgment of mind and choice was arbitrary. He had worked for many years without taking them into account. Then somehow, he imagined he had proved their nonexistence.

In 1972, he wrote:

> Beliefs, preferences, perceptions, needs, purposes and opinions are other possessions of autonomous man which are said to change when we change minds. What is changed in each case is a probability of action.[48]

Nothing more than that? What an assertion! It was like closing one's eyes and then announcing that one has proved the universe does not exist. Skinner and the behaviorists also imagined that they had disproved the existence of choice. Eventually Skinner came to regard those who believe that people make choices as "showing signs of emotional instability" and even as dangerous. For Skinner and his followers, psychology has nothing to do with understanding mental processes. Among its ultimate purposes is to become able to induce people to act in desired ways, in ways that the behaviorists think are best for them. For instance, Skinner would use his system to solve "the serious problem which arises when young people refuse to serve in the armed forces and desert or defect to other countries." Not just the subject matter of psychology but its very purpose underwent change. Arthur Koestler, whose book *Ghost in the Machine* contains a brilliant analysis of behaviorism, summed up this particular error as follows:

> At first the intention of behaviorism was merely to exclude consciousness, images and other nonpublic phenomena as *objects of study* from the field of psychology; but later on this came to imply that the excluded phenomena *did not exist.* A programme for a methodology, which had its arguable points, became transformed into a philosophy which had no point at all. One might as well tell a team of land surveyors that for the purpose of mapping a limited area they could treat the earth as if it were flat—and then subtly instill the dogma that the whole world is flat. [Koestler's italics.]

Had Skinner put forth the idea of determinism merely as an idea, his book *Beyond Freedom and Dignity* probably would not have attracted attention. The speculation is an old one. Fatalism was a theory that the ancient Greeks liked to play with, and versions of determinism have been put forth in every culture. James had considered the possibility and found it a fruitless hypothesis. But Skinner asserted, and apparently actually came to imagine, that he had discovered the nonexistence of mind and choice. Not that he presented any experimental evidence for such a discovery. He merely asserted the idea once again, only this time as if it were a fresh finding.

Skinner's thesis is simple enough. Since organisms do not exercise choice, all control is exercised by the environment. Skinner promises that by changing the environment in ways behaviorists will discover, we can develop absolute control over behavior. By giving the right doses of positive reinforcement we can cause people to act unfailingly as we want them to, and by giving negative or no reinforcement to undesirable behavior we can cause them to stop. By this method, Skinner assures us, he can get all human beings to behave in desirable ways and create an ideal society. His most impressive experiments thus far have been to train a certain breed of rat to press a bar predictably to get food, and to train pigeons to strut about and stretch their necks unnaturally high and perform simple acts for grain. From such imperfect control over *certain* behavior of *certain* organisms, he promises the prediction and control of all human behavior.

The pointlessness of using lower animals as subjects has been underscored by ethologists, whose specialty is the study of the way animal species survive. They observe that many species simply don't conform to the rules of behavior that seem to hold for others. They list their own animal experiments, which "represent a clear and utter failure of conditioning theory," and ironically give them the category "the misbehavior of organisms." As a leading ethologist put it, the work of the behaviorists is "overenthusiastic environmentalism":

> Humans are animals, perhaps very special animals, but animals nonetheless. Just as the other fauna of this planet are the products of organic evolution and are now being understood in this framework, humans evolved and deserve understanding in this context. But the promise that research in animal behavior will illuminate human behavior is over a century old, and remains unfilled. We have no animal-based science of human behavior despite the assemblage of suspect analogies.[41]

Behaviorists have thus far paid little attention to ethology, though there has been implicit recognition of the difficulties in generalizing from one species to another. For this reason they have been careful in choosing which animals to experiment with. What has been discovered about rats seems difficult to apply to mice, for instance. The latter are seldom used for study because they do not condition well. One behaviorist told me that mice were "too emotional." Until findings can be carried over from rats to mice, it seems rather blithe to insist that work with rats is sufficient to explain human behavior.

Still, Skinner feels able to announce that behavioristic principles discovered on lower animals will be applied successfully to all mankind's problems. For example, he remarks that we may be disturbed by the fact that so many young people work as little as possible. He then assures us that we "shall not get far by inspiring a sense of craftsmanship or pride in one's work or a sense of the dignity of labor." [1] These are for him meaningless concepts, and he puts them in quotations whenever he mentions them, as if to show that he wants nothing to do with them. Instead, the solution he offers is to reinforce the behavior we want, by which he means to *give* people something for the desired behavior and to withhold it if the behavior is not the desired one. Skinner even promises that by reinforcements he can get artists and poets to do better work and can produce an artistic society. He always regards reinforcement as something he will give to those who have performed. By his own system he has ruled out the possibility that the emergence of the poem or painting, its very happening, might be real reinforcements, that these inner states provide the true motivation for people to strive and to repeat performances that have brought them success.

One wonders how the Skinnerians would induce artists to do better work. Would they talk to the artists about their feelings, using verbal reports as part of their encouragement? How will they arrive at a way of measuring beauty? And if they don't, how can they say scientifically that a work of art is beautiful? Who would judge the artists? No answers are offered by the behaviorists. Only the claim is made.

Skinner tries to be consistent with his position that organisms respond to the environment and not their experience of the environment. For instance, he maintains that at the ballet when we want an encore we applaud the dancer. The applause induces him to dance again. In this respect Nureyev is no different from a toy we wind up when we want it to perform again. For Skinner, we, the audience, are controlling the dancer. Think how much is lost by this explanation! Sometimes our bravos bring an encore, and at other times not. The same applause is a reinforcement on one occasion but not on another. Why? The dancer could tell us perhaps. He was fatigued. Or he himself felt that he danced badly. It was a matter of personal pride. Or he didn't like us. Possibly, if he felt we imagined we could control him like a toy, he would decide not to come back out, to prove to us, and perhaps to himself, that he was *not* controllable. In any event, we are unable to understand him without a knowledge of his inner state. Very likely our attitude toward the dancer, if we were like Skinnerians and regarded him as without an inner life, would give us *less* authority over his behavior than a naively appreciative audience has. Far from controlling people, behaviorists, by their policy of devaluating people, often find themselves with less sway over them than they would otherwise have.

In spite of its efforts to be scientific, behaviorism relies on ill-defined verbal concepts, which result in circular and meaningless statements. One of these is the concept of reinforcement, a cornerstone of the whole system. It is actually defined in terms of itself. Skinner has put forth as a discovery that if an act is followed by presentation of a (positive) reinforcement, the organism tends to perform that act more often. But a reinforcement has been defined as a stimulus that gets the organism to act. As Koestler maintained, this results in a perfectly circular and meaningless statement:

> Translated into human language, we arrive at the tautology: the probability of repeating an action is increased by reinforcement, where 'reinforcement' means something which increases that probability.

Many other writers have pointed out the tautological nature of the so-called law of reinforcement. In addition, Noam Chomsky has observed that behaviorists do not even take seriously the requirement that a reinforcement be an identifiable stimulus. If a person continues to perform an act with no evident reinforcement, neither Skinner nor the other behaviorists hesitate to assert that there must have been a reinforcement *somewhere*, or the person would not have gone on. The meaninglessness of their concept of reinforcement protects behaviorists against disproof of statements in which it is used.

Certain of their concepts betray the failure of behaviorists to get away from the concept of mind, in spite of their meticulous efforts. As the neurophysiologist Robert Efron noted, mind is implicit in all discussions of reflex.[1] For what is a reflex but an act conducted without consciousness or volition? To use the term *reflex* as a classification is to imply the existence of other behavior *not* reflexive. Moreover, even the most rigorous behaviorists succumb to using the term *voluntary*. For instance, H. J. Eysenck, considered perhaps the most outstanding authority on behavior therapy, wrote the following: "We shall assume here that the term 'therapy' . . . should be reserved for instances where the patient voluntarily seeks treatment."

Eysenck, like certain other behavior therapists, resorted to use of the term *voluntary* to deal with charges of brainwashing. Certain methods of behavior therapy, those which cause the patient to suffer intensely, had been likened to methods used in the Inquisition. Often they were tried out on people incarcerated or at their wit's end. The defense offered by behavioral therapists was that the patient chose the therapy voluntarily.

Efron has also observed a curious fallacy in the behaviorists' refusal to study mental events. Behaviorists originally gave as their reason the belief that all such events will ultimately be describable in terms of physics and chemistry. But suppose this were so. What laws of consciousness is the physicist to explain? There would need to be study on both sides before we could match mental processes with the discoveries made about events in the physical universe. How can you account biologically for a fantasy, for instance, if you don't know what a fantasy is? "A reductionist, in order to succeed, would have to know the 'laws of consciousness' before he could know that he had explained them or deduced them from the 'laws of physics.' "

How do behaviorists proceed when in the role of therapist? How can they imagine they can solve a personal problem without even considering its psychological aspects? Yet when a patient wants to discuss his inner life, many actually discourage him. When someone comes to the therapist with an emotional problem, it is regarded as a "behavioral disturbance." The person is simply acting too much in certain ways and not enough in others. According to the theory that all behavior is controlled by externals, the therapist's aim is to devise an environment that will reinforce desired behavior and extinguish what he calls "maladaptive responses." On the theory that "maladaptive" behavior always results from its being positively reinforced, his primary method is to remove such reinforcements. In addition, he seeks to attach positive reinforcement to "adaptive behavior," which is the kind he wants to encourage.

Behavioral therapists maintain that their method enables them to disregard their patient's inner lives. By limiting themselves to externals, it is contended, they save a great deal of time. From their point of view, what does it matter why the patient thinks he feels certain ways? Or what the patient thinks his motivations are? The only real reasons for behavior are its external rewards and punishments—what the behaviorist calls its "contingencies." Behavioral therapy consists essentially of regulating these contingencies.

Typical was the following procedure reported in 1965 by a behavioral therapist. Israel Goldiamond saw a young couple whose marriage was in trouble. The husband told Goldiamond that his wife "had committed the 'ultimate betrayal' " two years previously with his best friend. "Since that time, whenever he saw his wife, he screamed at her for hours on end or else was ashamed of himself for having done so and spent hours sulking and brooding."

The therapist took as his essential purpose to stop the husband from shouting at the woman. This, as he saw it, was the harmful behavior, the nub of the problem. Why she had the affair, why it tormented her husband, whether she wanted another, whether it was the real issue, whether the couple should remain together or wanted to, whether the real problem lay elsewhere and was being displaced—no discussion of such questions was reported. The sulking and brooding were not considered as possible manifestations of something more important. The therapist, true to his behavioral premise, saw his purpose as simply to terminate the behavior that he considered to be the essential harm.

It appeared that the less the husband yelled, the more he sulked. To curtail his sulking, the husband was instructed that if he wished to sulk, he should do it in the garage on a special stool and stay there as long as he wished. He was also instructed to keep a record of the time spent sulking. Only after he finished was he to return to his wife. His sulking decreased as treatment progressed.

At least several times the husband objected to the superficiality of the approach. As part of the procedure he was stopped in his tracks when he showed curiosity about his inner life or his past:

> During the course of one of the sessions, he started to talk about his childhood, and was summarily cut off.
> "Shouldn't I talk about this with a psychologist?" he asked. "Isn't this one of the things that interests you? Doesn't it affect me now?"

The request must have been a keen insult to Goldiamond, who is a psychologist. However, he explained to the patient that his past was unimportant, using an analogy about a defective bridge. It was built weakly in the past, but it breaks because it cannot support a weight in the present.

That silenced the patient. The therapist recommended various environmental changes as part of his cure. For instance, "as part of the program of establishing new stimuli, the subject was instructed to rearrange the use of rooms and furniture in his house to make it appear considerably different. His wife went one step further and took the occasion to buy herself a new hat."

Later on the therapist asked if there was any topic of conversation that, once started, would maintain itself. The husband answered that discussing his mother-in-law's crazy ideas about farming was such a topic. The therapist then gave him an index card and instructed him to write "farm" on it and to attach a $20 bill to the card. The money was to pay for dinner out the following Thursday, after which they were to start a "farm" discussion, which it was to be hoped would continue in the taxi and at home.

Since there were sexual problems occurring in the bedroom, the therapist sought a "stimulus which could alter the room entirely." Finally, he had the couple install a yellow night light that they were to turn on when both felt amorous and that was to be kept off otherwise.

One wonders why the therapist chose yellow, and whether the use of the light was in any way derived from experiments done to get chickens to lay more eggs. The patient wanted his wife to be more helpless. The therapist told him that "if he wished his wife to act helpless, he should reinforce dependency by doing what she asked."

Think about the oversimplification of this approach. One problem was the husband's unhappiness, which he expressed by sulking. Possibly the sulking had other meanings, too, and was only one way he conveyed his unhappiness. But the behavioral therapist disregarded the patient's state of unhappiness as a problem, because on principle he did not talk about inner states. Then, having gotten the person to sulk less, he was able to conclude that he had solved the essential problem. For all we know, the husband was just as miserable, or more so, after the therapy was over.

In the same article Goldiamond reported a second case in which a couple came to him after being married for 10 years. Throughout their marriage they had had sexual relations only about twice a year, and they agreed that this had been due to the husband. Being Roman Catholics, they were determined to stay married, but the wife thought she might be driven into extramarital relations.

Goldiamond recommended that they read *Playboy* "to initiate amorous activity," but the husband fell asleep reading it. The therapist explained the principles of behavior therapy to them, which they understood. Later the wife volunteered, "I am at my wit's end as to how to shape his behavior. I don't know what reinforcements I have. I could withhold supper, but that is not a good reinforcer because I can't turn it off and on. I can't apply deprivation, because that's my problem. I don't know what to do."

The therapist then suggested that the husband schedule his wife in his appointment book for two evenings a week. But they kept these appointments for only two weeks. An analysis of how they felt might have explained why they stopped meeting each other, but such introspective work is not part of behavior therapy. The only conclusion Goldiamond could draw is that meeting each other was not sufficiently reinforced. Then came the search for reinforcements that could induce them to meet. Both the husband and wife were well groomed, he frequently going to a barber and she to a beautician. The husband suggested "that they might attach the opportunity to visit the beautician or barber as consequences to keeping appointments." If they broke an appointment, the visits would not be allowed. Both felt that this would be effective. As a result of these reinforcements, they continued seeing each other for the rest of the semester. Goldiamond's report does not say whether anything else was accomplished, but he wrote up the case presumably to illustrate his method.

What restraint it must take for the therapist to refrain from asking questions of decided relevance! "Mrs. X, how do you feel knowing that your husband keeps appointments with you only to get to see his barber?" Nearly any non-behavioral therapist with any reasonable degree of training and insight would see such a question as necessary. It is as if the behaviorist by his position makes himself an utter outsider, unable to pursue lines of inquiry that would be available to anyone else. Perhaps the husband's suggestion was made in anger. Perhaps he knew that such a suggestion would hurt his wife's feelings. It was as if to say, "You mean nothing to me, but for a barber appointment, I'll meet you." If this was the case, why was he angry? Does he often express anger so indirectly?

Or if not, can the joy of a haircut really generalize to sexual pleasure with an unwanted wife? From what experiences do we generalize? Behaviorists seem to assume that we generalize from any kind of reinforcement. But do we have sexual feelings about the person who brings us food when we're hungry?

The accounts of these two attempts at treatment are more damning than anything one could say about them. It cannot be that this sort of method is to replace all the discoveries made about the mind over the centuries. Have all our playwrights and novelists been on an utterly wrong track with their understanding of motivation?

It seems evident that behavioral therapy, at least of this kind, is misguided. In fact, it's hard to imagine that even Goldiamond believes in it. More likely, to give him credit, he was pursuing a hypothesis. How would he feel knowing that his own wife needed a beautician's appointment to spend time with him? Or, for instance, that his children needed the reward of toys? Surely it would not satisfy him. There is a world of difference between someone's feeling desire to be with you and their doing it to get something else of value. Perhaps if it took bribes to induce his loved ones to spend time with him, Goldiamond would question whether something was wrong with him. It would be wise to generalize and assume at least the possibility that, in spite of her seeming confidence, the wife he was treating also felt shaken about her worth. We all know that it matters *why* people want to be with us. There is no sense pretending the issue is irrelevant, just to avoid having to refer to people's inner lives.

Two questions, which we are to answer later on, arise in connection with the behaviorists' work. The first concerns the exact relevance of a person's past history. The second has to do with the real meaning of symptoms.

Can it profit a patient to know the origin of his problem? The behaviorists have decided it cannot. Theirs is an acute counterreaction to the position taken by psychoanalysis, as has been already mentioned. Freud held that there could be no cure until past causes were comprehended—no going forward without going back. Behaviorists counter by saying that knowledge of how a problem began is unnecessary for either the patient or the therapist.

Behaviorists raise the question of what a *symptom* means and whether in fact there is such a thing. Psychoanalysis regards the inner lives of people as supplying their true motive force, and as giving rise to their behavior. The mental mechanism determines behavior. What the patient does is a symptom of his underlying condition. According to this view, there is no point in getting a patient to act differently. Since all his actions are merely symptoms of an underlying condition that is constant, if you stifle one symptom, another will appear in its place. The behaviorists' reaction to this has been to deny the existence of symptoms altogether. Behavior is not symptomatic but the essence of personality. Behaviorists deny the phenomenon that the analysts call "the switching of symptoms." However, the phenomenon of replacement is real and has often been observed. Here a quote from Goldiamond's first report becomes relevant: "Since in the absence of yelling at his wife, the subject sulked and since the program was designed to reduce yelling, the subject's sulking was in danger of increasing."

This is exactly what psychoanalysts mean by the switching

of symptoms. In their view, the inner state has manifested itself by giving rise to a new symptom.

Reinforcement methods have proved helpful in particular cases to which behaviorists have ingeniously applied them. For instance, certain autistic children are prone to mutilate their own bodies. By administering a small number of electric shocks to the extremities in response to such behavior, behavioral researchers have been able to terminate it. Behaviorists have also been able to discover when and how often to apply negative reinforcements. But those instances in which negative reinforcement proves helpful are limited compared to the wide range of problems to which reinforcement techniques are applied.

Their obvious inability to cure people's problems wholly by attaching measurable reinforcements to observable behavior has long been evident to many behavioral researchers, as has their inability to develop techniques on lower animals and apply them to humans. Behavior therapists writing up their reports do not as a rule even bother to mention animal studies. And those who work with animals pay little or no attention to behavioral therapy with humans. As one outstanding behaviorist observed: "The majority of psychologists now active understand that there is a great deal more to human and animal learning than reinforcement of overt behavior or conditioning more generally." [31]

The failure of behaviorism to produce a scientific system that bypasses inner life has not discouraged use of the term. Researchers calling themselves behavior therapists have devised a variety of techniques using their knowledge of people and their own experiences, techniques that assume inner states and that are utterly unscientific by their own criteria. For instance, some now regard thinking and feeling as "covert behavior" and thus can talk about such immeasurables while retaining the title of behaviorist. They also use what they call "controlled fantasy." An example would be proposing to a patient that he imagine an undesirable action that he engages in, and at the same time entertain an extremely unpleasant thought. For instance, it has been suggested that the person try to think of rotten eggs while picturing a lover one wants to fall out of love with.

Two surveyors of these methods have concluded: "Behavioral methods are loaded with affective and cognitive variables of the same kind that dominate other therapies." [7] Translated, this means that these behaviorists are trying to integrate thoughts and feelings into their system.

Utilizing a wide variety of methods they call behavioral, some behaviorists have doubtless helped particular patients. For instance, behavioral therapists sometimes teach assertiveness by modeling the behavior themselves. They show the patient how to say no, how to express his feelings, and so forth. This would seem valuable for certain people, especially those whose problems stem from their not having had good models. However, many timid people require more than a good example to follow. They are timid mainly because they had an overwhelming example of assertiveness in a parent. Other behavioral therapists teach their patient how to relax, borrowing methods from a variety of sources. Though this is not down to a science yet, it appears to work with some people. So far no single method of relaxation has demonstrated clear superiority over the others.

The point is that, having disdained insight therapy of all kinds, behavioral therapists now resort to it. It is becoming increasingly difficult each year to distinguish behavior therapy from certain others. Thus two commentators on the field wrote:

> Insight therapies of all types address themselves to the rationality of the patient, and behavioral therapies direct their operations to the sensorimotor level, but all therapies work through the medium of an actual or implied human relationship whose manifest and convincing purpose must be to help the patient.[32]

By what criteria does this "human relationship" qualify as behavioristic? And could it not be argued that psychoanalysis and every other form of talk therapy address themselves to the "sensorimotor level"? After all, the purpose of insight is not merely to know but also to change the way we feel about ourselves and the ways we act.

By now behaviorists are using such terms as "ego strength" and "subjective anxiety." They even talk about warmth and empathy. However, they often refer to feelings as "affective responses," imagining the use of such terms makes them scientific. Behavioral techniques are constantly changing. None convinces the majority, or even a sizable minority, of its validity.

The use of myriad unproven techniques by insight therapists, none of which is acceptable to the majority, is not surprising. It was to clear up such diversity that the decision was made by behaviorists to become scientific. However, since science was the chief claim of behaviorists, and since much else was sacrificed for it, their failure to agree on what has already been established is deplorable.

The reviewers of the field wrote in the *Annual Review of Psychology*, after delving into more than a thousand files of published research:

> We seem to know how to intervene successfully, but from an experimental sense, we may not be able to specify precisely or conclusively the crucial variables involved in such intervention. Our salvation, of course, is that such a dilemma may be simply inherent in the field of therapy, whether it be behavior therapy or psychotherapy, for both suffer equally.[7]

Rather than admit that behavioral therapy failed in its promise to help people by purely objective means, behavioral therapists are trying to help people in other ways. And the ways they choose are nearly always methods devised by insight therapists. In other words, they rely heavily for their techniques on work done by others, who believe that people think and feel and that many psychological problems cannot be measured by techniques used in other sciences.

Behaviorism has failed utterly in its original promise, and most behavioral therapists know it. One researcher, A. A. Lazarus, canvassed 20 behavioral therapists who were in personal therapy themselves. His article was titled, "Where Do Behavior Therapists Take Their Troubles?" Half were going to psychoanalysts and the rest to therapists of various orientations. Not a single one was himself being treated by a behavior therapist! Among their explanations were the following remarks: "My therapist is a beautiful human being and that means more to me than his theoretical orientation." "Let's face it, if you can afford it in terms of time and money, psychoanalysis is still the treatment of choice."

For one reason or another, they apparently felt they deserved better treatment than their own patients were getting. Like Goldiamond's patient, they wanted to go to a real psychologist, presumably one who would take them seriously.

Each year new techniques are devised, and behavioral therapy continues to exist, but in new forms. There is relatively little cross-validation research, and results are published after very short follow-up periods. In reporting their successes, behaviorists allow even less time than when other disciplines report theirs. One research team actually reported that controlled drinking was as good an attack on alcoholism as total abstinence for the same period. The report was made after a six-month follow-up.[53] But Alcoholics Anonymous, an organization that has cured a million alcoholics in 75 countries, has found the opposite and is able to do follow-ups after 20 years and sometimes after 30 or more. The routine practice of writing follow-up reports shortly after treatment tends to keep claims alive. There always seems something new on the horizon. But, to say the least, the success claims of behavior therapists are greatly overstated.

Behaviorism has added its color to the spectrum of therapies. Its emphasis on people's behavior as *not* a superficial phenomenon is important. It surely has been a corrective to claims that contemporary behavior is nothing more than a manifestation of inner states. As for the claims made by certain behaviorists that they can control all human behavior, these need not be taken too seriously. Behaviorists do not possess the means to follow through on this threat. The power of the voluntary is great, and it is not possible to control people's minds against their will. Besides, the majority of behaviorists now practicing do not share such a desire.

Behaviorists have taken a position on several other forms of therapy and used them. Some have studied the writings of Carl Rogers, who believes that warmth and acceptance, in themselves, are curative. Rogers believes that we have a "self-actualizing potential": The experience of being fully accepted by someone will, he believes, lead us to accept ourselves and this in itself is all we need. He has trained many students in what he calls "nondirective therapy," which he conceives of as a very subtle art of bringing out the patient's present experience without exerting any influence on the patient to become a particular kind of person. For Rogers the patient does the diagnosis and sets all the goals, and the patient provides the cure. The behaviorists believe that by his responses the therapist is actually influencing the patient, positively reinforcing the patient in particular directions. There has been a growing interest in Rogers's work, which behaviorists reinterpret as a subtle but effective system of reinforcement.

Behaviorists are, of course, committed to the denial of Freud's basic principles—such ideas as the ones that sexuality is behind nearly everything, that the past needs to be relived, that character congeals. For this reason they consider it almost treasonous to delve into the psychoanalytic literature. But psychoanalysis is much more than a body of speculative theory. Freud and his followers have made an enormous number of discoveries that should not be overlooked. The early psychoanalysts and those that followed them were imaginative and sensitive people who acquired an enormous amount of information about how people think and act. Now that behaviorists are becoming introspective themselves, they owe it to their own development to reconsider many topics that psychoanalysts have already gone into in depth. What are the characteristics of different kinds of attitudes? When are patients resisting treatment, and how is one to deal with the various kinds of resistance? How does the patient view the therapist? And how may such knowledge be used to understand the patient better? What feelings does the patient induce in the therapist? Psychoanalysts have been concerning themselves with such questions for more than half a century, and they have made numerous discoveries that it would be foolhardy to neglect.

For instance, what feelings did Goldiamond have when his patient actually asked to see a psychologist? Behavioral therapists are not strictly supposed to consider the feelings that the patient evokes in the therapist or their relevance to treatment. This is the very stuff that psychoanalysis has been studying from the beginning. Not to go into this subject matter leaves one open to many pitfalls, and indeed such material is often the most crucial for cure. At this early stage in their thinking about mind, behavioral therapists are subject to all the errors that long ago led psychoanalysts to examine themselves closely as a precondition to their becoming therapists.

Although many behavioral therapists now acknowledge the existence of mind, they still pay heavily for the premises from which their founding fathers denied its existence. They have every right to reinterpret observations as they see fit, and naturally they cannot be expected to arrive at Freudian conclusions. But it ought not to be anathema for anyone doing therapy to delve into Freud's writings or to refer to his discoveries. Behavioral therapists are cheating themselves and forcing themselves in the long run to retrace many of the steps that Freud and his followers took more than half a century ago.

With behaviorism, psychology has become less speculative. But in the process it has surrendered much of its interest in the countless mysteries of the mind that it originally sought to study. It banished from the field many figments of the imagination. But some of psychology's speculations were prompted by real discoveries that have also been given short shrift. It is true that reality ought to be enough to occupy us. But when it comes to mental events, we simply cannot insist that unless others see them they do not exist. Nor has behaviorism given us any reason to disbelieve in the power of what some of us fondly call "human will."

Behaviorism thus suggests leaving far behind the systematic study of people as initiators who might ultimately have much to say about their own personality and outlook on life.

CHAPTER FIVE

The Instinct Argument

Cried this pretentious Ape one day,
  "I'm going to be a Man!
And stand upright, and hunt, and fight,
  And conquer all I can!
I'm going to cut down forest trees,
  And make my houses higher!
I'm going to kill the Mastodon!
  I'm going to make a fire!"

Loud screamed the Anthropoidal Apes
  With laughter wild and gay;
. . . Most conclusive and admitting no reply,
You would have to change your nature!
  We should like to see you try!"

They chuckled then triumphantly,
  These lean and hairy shapes,

> *For these things passed as arguments*
> *With the Anthropoidal Apes.*
> from "Similar Cases"
> Charlotte Stetson Gilman

From one last battery of experts comes the thesis of human helplessness. There are those who maintain that our behavior is dictated by our genes, and hence that we cannot change our nature. This would imply the impossibility, or at least the serious limitations, of a psychology seeking to give people control over the construction of their psyche.

The majority of geneticists and of animal researchers would doubtless not wish to comment on the question of whether there is an inherent human nature. However, the ideas of a few popularizers have caught the public fancy in recent years. And though some of these ideas are exciting to think about, in the sense that it is exciting to hear a sentence of doom, none has any solid evidence behind it. These assertions contribute to a general sense of fatalism, widely prevalent, as well as justifying further the lassitude within psychology about studying human possibility.

Contemporary instinct theorists argue that certain inherited dispositions are in our makeup because long ago we needed them for survival. For instance, Konrad Lorenz, whose research on animals has been widely publicized, regards the aggressive drive as having a destructive intensity in human beings. Lorenz believes that this "aggressive urge" has been bred into human beings over tens of thousands of years and talks of it as including particular forms of behavior on our part. Another, Niko Tinbergen, argues that man still carries with him the animal heritage of group territoriality. Human beings instinctively band together in groups to fight outsiders. He sees in wars the fusion of the aggressive and the territorial urges, describing them in what he calls a "biological perspective."

For Robert Ardrey the critical instinct we inherit is "hatred of strangers." Ardrey maintains that, because of this instinct, "we must invent strangers." Other instincts whose existence is posited by contemporary writers include those of hoarding, mother love, the impulse to hunt, the striving for rank and status and even our desire to speak up. Lorenz has argued that we inherit particular adult ways of feeling toward young children, which are provoked by the sight of certain physical traits, such as a large head in proportion to the body, large eyes in the middle of the total head, and even by behavioral cues such as the clumsiness of the infant.

These writers vary in their beliefs regarding the human capacity to surmount instincts. Most tend to think we cannot. For instance, Tinbergen writes: "Lorenz is, in my opinion, right in claiming that the elimination, through education, of the internal urge to fight will turn out to be very difficult, if not impossible."

And Ardrey has maintained that even if we can stop ourselves from going to war, this will merely invoke an inner necessity to express our hostility toward one another elsewhere. "Human violence, once fulfilled on the battlefield, is today being fulfilled in the city's streets." He actually makes the case for the preferability of warfare, since it unites societies and "gives outlet for animal xenophobia."

Some maintain that instincts govern our everyday social behavior. One writer has asserted that inborn territoriality is behind the custom of giving a present to someone when visiting that person at home. It is to assuage the violation of entering his territory. And the custom of asking permission to sit down in a partially occupied train compartment, he maintains, is again testimony to a mutual sense of territory.

That physical space and privacy have value is beyond question—the question is whether the desire for them is inherited or evolves out of experience.

On what basis do these writers believe that human behavior is determined by instinct? Nearly always, their argument rests on the examination of the behavior of lower species. The earliest discoveries of territoriality, for instance, came from observations made by ornithologists. Most bird species are territorial. In some species, individuals guard a territory; in others, pairs do, and in still other species a whole group protects its space. Most fish are also territorial, and so are many varieties of land animals. Each of the other traits that these writers have attributed to humans have been found to appear as unlearned characteristics of particular species. Members of the species, even reared in isolation, will predictably display the particular trait. The squirrel will hoard; the ape will be xenophobic; the eagle, the hyena, and the lion will guard their territory, and so forth.

Animal researchers have demonstrated beyond question that there are innate behavior patterns that come to maturity in lower animals—patterns that would, if found in humans, justify their "instinct theories." For instance, D. A. Spalding raised swallows in cages so small they could not flap their wings. There was no chance to copy others or to practice flying. Yet when given the chance, the birds could immediately fly. Even more relevant are discoveries of what ethologists call the "fixed action pattern." This is defined as a sequence of coordinated motor actions that appears without the animal's having to learn it by the usual learning processes. The animal can perform the behavior without previous exercise and without having seen another member of its species do it. The fixed action pattern is constant in form, which means that the sequence of motor actions never varies.

The great advantage of having fixed action patterns is that the animal does not run risks during a trial-and-error period. It acts in a way that is helpful to its survival on the very first occasion it is given the chance to do so. Both Lorenz and Tinbergen have done pioneer work in discovering such patterns in subhuman species. They have demonstrated beyond question the presence of what they call "releasing mechanisms." The animal releases the particular behavior when certain stimuli are present. Included are acts analogous to mother love, territoriality, xenophobia, and even the offspring's tendency to stay in close contact with a parent. In many lower species such behavior is not learned, and yet the creature predictably acts as its species does. Ethologists do not maintain that it comes into existence with any fore-knowledge of its environment. It has no prophetic inklings of what the earth will be like or of who will occupy it. What it inherits, in the organization of its nervous system, is a complex way of behaving that, under usual circumstances, helps it to survive.

The argument that human beings must have inherited the necessity for certain behavior is based on what is called "the doctrine of phylogenetic continuity." Such mechanisms have been passed down over the ages through all our mam-malian ancestors. True, they become fewer as one ascends in the animal kingdom. The wasp is more a victim of neces-sity in its behavior than the wolf, and the wolf more than the chimpanzee. Instinctivists argue that these mechanisms must also dominate human behavior to some extent.

Usually, the phylogenetic argument is supported by ob-servations of human behavior. Human beings often do many of the same things that animals do. Most mothers care for their young. Humans hoard, band together and fight for territory, and so forth. Instinct theorists sometimes account for these similarities by saying that, like lower animals, humans have been programmed to act in these ways. Many instinct theorists base their case almost entirely on what they observe of human behavior. They see, or imagine they see, universal tendencies in human behavior, and to them it seems most plausible to assume that such behavior must be instinctive.

There's nothing illogical in the idea of a phylogenetic con-tinuity of instincts. If a bird does something always, a monkey often, and people sometimes, then conceivably an instinct is at work. The human simply has the least amount of it. But there's no logical necessity to believe in such a continuity. Birds fly and we don't, not even a little. Besides, it isn't so simple as the record of some kinds of behavior diminishing as we go up a clear-cut ladder. For instance, territoriality diminishes sharply in some species and then becomes greater in others, as we go up the phylogenetic scale. Great apes, for instance, are not at all territorial.

Besides, it is one thing to allow the possibility of instinctive activity in humans and another to imagine that any example of it has been found. It's merely a speculation that the doctrine of phylogenetic continuity applies to humans in such a way that it governs behavior, that the tendencies we inherit are truly more powerful than we are in controling us.

As the animal researcher Frank Beach noted, instinct theories applied to human behavior represent the *nominal fallacy*. This fallacy is the confusion between explaining something and merely giving it a name. It is not an explanation of human hoarding, for example, to say merely that it represents an instinct to hoard. Nor does it explain wars to say that they are caused by an instinct to act aggressively or destructively. Every mature adult human behavior evolves as a consequence of so many factors, including learning, that no one can possibly know enough to pinpoint an underlying instinct for it. In other words, even if there were such inborn impulses in the human makeup as instinctivists assert, they would be unknowable. One would have to do experiments analogous to those Spaulding did with swallows, and for a variety of evident reasons such experiments are not likely to be done.

Closely related to the nominal fallacy is another kind of confusion, which unfortunately has been common in psychology. This is the fallacy of mistaking the *consequence* of behavior as having necessarily been its *intention*. Both Freud and Lorenz made this mistake. They concluded that because wars have haunted history, we must have in our mammalian heritage an inborn impulse for aggression, which leads to war. However, the fact that millions of people go to war, or find themselves in any kind of predicament, does not imply that they have sought it or wanted it unconsciously, or that they were programmed to want it. People often produce effects very different from those they intend. They are simply not in perfect control over all effects of their behavior. There is no reason to posit the lurking presence of an instinct for war from the fact of war, any more than an instinct for justice or for peace, though people with those ideals are also to be found nearly everywhere. There is still absolutely no experimental evidence showing the presence of instincts in people. What Frank Beach once said still holds:

> It is important to note that this war over instinct was fought more with words and inferential reasoning than with behavioral evidence. . . . Most of the battles of the campaign were fought from the armchair in the study rather than from the laboratory.

Since the time of his making this observation in 1955, experimental studies of lower animals have been done in abundance. And the evidence has been that there are even more remarkable differences between species than was thought. The statement nonetheless applies as well today as it did when written, regarding any discussion of instincts in human beings. Neither the psychoanalysts nor the animal researchers, such as Lorenz and Tinbergen, have any special knowledge of human behavior that would warrant their conclusions. Concerning war, what they know they derived from reading newspaper accounts, like the rest of us. They have no experimental evidence to demonstrate inborn tendencies of the kind they suppose. They are merely conjecturing about human behavior.

Besides, as was mentioned, one can find examples of every conceivable kind of behavior in the animal kingdom. It is not true, as Ardrey asserts, that territoriality is ever-present among animals. Bisons, antelopes, and horses form large herds, and territorial jealousy is unknown to them. The chimpanzee is neither territorial nor xenophobic but lives in an open society in which strangers are greeted amiably and even enthusiastically. There is so much variety in the animal kingdom that it makes no sense to single out a species and draw conclusions about human beings on the basis of its behavior. The variety is unending. Those who attribute instincts to humans after studying the patterns of lower species commit the same kind of error that moralists did who used animals as exemplars. With the conclusion in mind, they choose the animal to serve as their example.

The only statement we can make with impunity is that certain human behavior *reminds* us of particular animal behavior. For instance, a person who hoards his money is reminiscent of a squirrel, a protective parent reminds us of many animals who dote upon their young, and so forth.

Anthropologists, as our foremost experts at debunking universals, have been enormously influential in adducing evidence against those instinct theories put forth. Perhaps more than anyone else, anthropologists have made us aware of the different styles of human behavior, all of which feel natural to those who engage in them.

For example, there are tribes in which "mother love" seems not to be the rule. The Mundugumor tribeswomen openly detest bearing their children and rearing them and leave much of the care of children to the men. Even the so-called instinct of self-preservation seems weak or non-existent in some places. The anthropologist Ruth Benedict has noted that in certain American Indian tribes, suicide is a light matter, the recourse of anyone who has suffered some slight rebuff. And there are tribes that apparently know nothing of war. Of one group Benedict wrote:

> I myself tried to talk of warfare to the Mission Indian of California, but it was impossible. Their misunderstanding of warfare was abysmal. They did not have the basis in their own culture upon which the idea could exist.

As Benedict put it, and as contemporary anthropologists would agree:

> Those explanations of custom which derive our eco-

nomic scheme from human competitiveness, modern war from human combativeness, and all the rest of the ready explanations that we meet in every magazine and modern volume, have for the anthropologist a hollow ring.

Anthropologists point out that there are drastic differences in shifting from one society to another, and there are often stunning differences in values and behavior between two neighboring societies. Moreover, anthropologists have observed radical changes in the same society, which obviously could not be accounted for by chromosomal changes in the members. To almost all anthropologists, any attempt to account for human activity by instincts is unwarranted.

Conceivably, there is a hint of instinct in our makeup. No one can disprove this possibility—just as we are nowhere near proving it. It is not crucial for anthropology to deny the possibility. So far, it merely asserts that no evidence for instinct has been found in the study of human activity. There are what anthropologists call "cradle traits," which date back to time immemorial and seem ubiquitous. Do we all undergo common situations and therefore some common learning? Anthropology can wonder with the rest of us, but the working hypothesis of anthropology is that culture is learned and transmitted, and that each has its individual integrity.

Doubtless there are biological elements in us that influence our temperament. These predispose us toward certain moods. But moods are quite separate from a person's character or outlook. One can express a temperamental disposition in totally various ways. As William James put it, aggression can be directed against poverty and disease and need not take any such form as competition or war. If there are unrestricted and limitless numbers of ways a person can express his temperament, then, though genes may influence our temperament, they do not determine how we actually behave. The choice of how to integrate our temperament into a total personality would remain ours. But being born with a necessity to act in particular ways would be another matter.

Surely inheritance plays a major role in our lives. We have inherited the complex physiology that marks us as human beings and not members of any other species. Much of its detail has been crucial for our survival over the three billion or so years since life on earth began. During the eons when ice covered Europe and people took refuge in caves, we survived because of certain characteristics, many of which we doubtless still possess. Time after time, the cruel logic of nature made selections among us. Unfortunates without the needed abilities were eliminated. Like our bodies, our minds are the result of a definite genetic endowment. Our mental faculties were bred in us by selection just as surely as our foreshortened faces and capacious craniums. But this is not the same as saying that we are programmed to engage irrevocably in fixed patterns of behavior.

Nothing in Darwin's work implies the necessity on our part to act in any highly defined way. Darwin himself speculated that certain styles of expression might be built into the human mechanism. For instance, he wrote that "extreme disgust is expressed by movements round the mouth identical with those preparatory to the act of vomiting." Regarding pride, he wrote that "a proud man exhibits his sense of superiority over others by holding his head and body erect. He is haughty, or high, and makes himself appear as large as possible." These Darwin thought might well be universal ways of expressing such emotions. He noted such modes of expression in far-removed cultures as well as in his own British society. He saw them in idiots and in those who were unlikely to have copied them. Perhaps he was right. Still, whether we feel pride or disgust is up to us. There are people dominated by pride and others full of disgust. Whether we feel one or the other, and why—these are the important issues. The behaviorists, by the way, have always acknowledged genetic contributions while believing that life experiences determine their expression. As Watson put it:

Every act has a genetic history. Take smiling. Our life history determines what we laugh at and who we laugh at.[61]

One person smiles at any mention of sex because it embarrasses him. Another smiles because he is full of hate, and his smiling relieves anger. What counts in our lives is not our style of smiling or our mode of expressing any particular emotion. What truly matters is whether and when we have particular reactions. If the individual has ultimate control over these, then instinct theories are misleading. All our behavior is the expression of attitudes we evolve in our lifetime by mechanisms we inherited. What we inherit is the equipment to become almost anything.

Other living creatures, limited to fixed patterns of behavior by the nature of their particular genetic endowments, use them in an effort to maximize their chances. They have their own remarkable traits by which they struggle to survive. There are many seeming miracles in nature. Bees, for instance, can see ultraviolet light. Bats can hear ultrasonic tones. Nile pike send out electrical impulses and react to the surrounding electrical field. Redbreasted robins utilize the earth's magnetic field for navigation. And one could go on and on. Humans can do none of these things. Our particular "miracle" is our ability to learn and our unparalleled ability to vary behavior, to be pliant.

To lose sight of this human faculty is to overlook the very strength that makes many things possible.

In these chapters, I've briefly described the descent of psychology. Originally designed as a body of learning that people could utilize to understand themselves and to change, psychology tended to lose its direction over time. Such loss came about partly because there were real difficulties in making progress, but also because at the start there seemed no reason to identify any special characteristics of psychology. It was as if a huge telescope were pointed in the right direction. Not a powerful one for all purposes, but well aimed. Gradually it swung away from its original aim, and psychology began to ask less important questions and to engage in fewer important pursuits. But this does not mean that the study of the human mind and will has reached a dead end.

PART TWO
The Study of Pliancy

There is no rock we can build on except the possibility of what we may become.

Sidney Hook

Think of pliancy not as a mere reaction to the environment but as a process that a person might control—as an ability that lies dormant. If it comes about as a result of choices we make, of controllable acts, then why could we not choose acts with the deliberate purpose of creating a particular outlook for ourselves? What is needed is the information that might teach us how to do this, and in this way to transcend environment.

Ordinarily, the child, and then the adult, acts with definite purposes in mind. Most of our concern is with how the act will affect the world. Because of this emphasis on exterior effects, people fail to appreciate how their choices affect themselves. The person doesn't say, "These acts will raise my self-esteem or reduce paranoia or enhance my appreciation of members of the opposite sex." As a result, by far the most significant effects of a person's choices—their cumulative impact on the personality itself—receive very little attention or none at all.

The study of pliancy aims at rectifying this, by uncovering exactly the knowledge that people actually need. With such knowledge, we can choose acts for their anticipated effects on ourselves. In this section I want to describe my pursuit of such knowledge.

CHAPTER SIX

Change versus Constancy

About fifteen years ago I began to study the question, Just how much control does the human being have over his vision of life?

What matters is how people affect themselves. Can people, by making the right choices at the right time, by some combination of voluntary acts, alter their basic way of feeling, of seeing, and of doing? Pliancy centers on how people influence themselves by controllable acts, and my purpose from the beginning was to identify any instances in which acts produce such effects. My hope was to collect enough so that I could generalize from them.

Almost from the beginning, it seemed that the best place to look was at unexpected changes in people, rather than at constancy. As for sameness, psychology had made it easy to use. Psychoanalysis has tirelessly pointed out people's unwitting consistency over a period of years. That a neglected and stingy child becomes a selfish adult was interesting, but what occurs when such a child turns into an open-handed and

89

confident adult was more interesting. If people stay the same, it remains an open question whether they are frozen that way or are unknowingly keeping themselves as they are. But where they change, there is the possibility for study of just what I was looking for. Correct principles should explain both change and sameness, but they could be identified only by studying change.

If I were ever to be able to draw generalizations and base a psychology on such effects, I would need examples in which people's own acts affected their mental state. At first, it was hard to think in terms of a person's producing an effect on his own outlook. I had been trained traditionally and had to remind myself to keep saying, "Now this seems like a change in someone's attitude. Is there anything the person himself has been doing that might have caused it?" Each time I could reasonably answer yes, I had an instance to note in my catalog that might lead me, inductively, to the generalizations I sought.

One of the first things I noticed was that if suspicious people got themselves to trust others even a little, after a while they nearly always would become less suspicious. Many therapists have noticed that if a patient trusts them more, as by confiding in them, the patient is almost sure to feel more trustful of them. This leaves open the possibility that the patient has simply tested the water and found it fit to navigate. In the case of one woman who took such a gamble with me, perhaps my own receptivity to her contributed to her confidence. But her trusting me, *her act*, was intrinsically important.

In another kind of case it seemed clearer that the patient's own behavior had caused the effect. The patient had changed despite receiving reactions that, if anything, might have discouraged change. A man of 57 in a profound depression told me that no one would hire someone his age. He was qualified to do freelance bookkeeping, and there were stores that sought the service he could offer. As I listened to his mournful conclusions I saw that there were two major strains in what he was saying. First, he was convinced that people would be *right* to turn him down, and might be warranted to despise someone so old for obtruding himself; second, he had doubts over whether he could do the job.

Just as with the woman, I encouraged the man to trust the world. In his case such trust meant applying for certain jobs. My assurances that not everyone felt as he anticipated had no real effect on his own expectation. He sometimes felt that he could handle the job and that people would be wrong to prejudge him. But this way of thinking was fragile and infrequent. Usually, he felt unworthy. It lightened the load a little for him to know that he could find solace in talking to me if he were turned down. With me on his side he was not as alone as he had been. After a time, with my assurances sounding like a broken record, he found the additional motivation to apply for some jobs and get rejected just to prove me wrong.

But actually his trying for jobs influenced his own thinking in a way that made me seem right.

During a two-week interval while I was out of town he lined up a few appointments. At one he was kept waiting and then refused. Several other interviewers told him the job was filled. Then a young and nattily dressed interviewer told him outright that he was too old—they had someone younger in mind—and refused even to let him take the written test for the job. While he was relating these events, I realized that they were the very ones he had anticipated with most dread. He could use them as confirmation that he had been right all along. I was getting ready to counter that conclusion and to encourage him about life in general, when I realized that he had experienced no such reaction.

On the contrary, he had altered his thinking in the very direction I had hoped for! His applying for the jobs had convinced him that people were wrong not to give him a chance and that 57 was not as old as they thought. He still felt uncertain about how well he could perform. He had been out of work for two years. But I noticed more than a hint of anger in his appraisal—anger toward the rather slangy young interviewers who would exclude people on the basis of age alone. He spoke with passion about a man much older who saved a corporation from bankruptcy and who, on the basis of age, would not have been offered the job either. By his own actions, trying for various jobs over a period of weeks, he had altered his perception. He had done for his own thinking something that I had been unable to do for him. My exhortations in comparison with his own efforts had the strength of a car's battery alongside that of its engine. Although the battery can get the car started, it can propel the car at most a foot or two by itself; only the engine can enable it to cover any sizable distance.

The case was notable to me then because the man had not received the kind of reinforcement that behaviorists say produces basic change. Some of his worst forebodings about how he might be treated were borne out, and yet he had greatly improved. His own striving had changed his attitude somewhat. If he'd been well received somewhere, perhaps I might not have realized this fact and would have mistakenly attributed his change to his being encouraged by some kindly interviewer. That was my first inkling of how greatly exaggerated the importance of outside reinforcements is. Incentives can obviously motivate us to act. But our purposeful actions are what alter our way of thinking, as this case and thousands of subsequent ones made clear to me.

Before long I had a notebook filled with instances in which people's own behavior changed their outlook. Often there had been tangible rewards for the new behavior that changed them. Yet it was evident that their striving, and not the rewards, had affected their mental state. In fact, in many instances I studied, the rewards actually interfered! I remember one early example of this that seemed clearer than the rest.

A woman had volunteered to help her boss out in an emergency. He had been kind to her and she felt glad for the chance. When he offered her money for the extra hours she had freely given, she refused it. Helping him had been good for her sense of dignity and was actually making the job better. Taking a reward might have diminished these benefits, which, fortunately, she sensed, and both of them gained by her declining it.

That rewards could actually *interfere* with the psychological benefit afforded by an act was worth noting. However, not for some years did I appreciate why this was so. It was one of many truths whose explanation was still not forthcoming.

My search for principles that might help foretell the effects of acts had gone on for a year. So far I had examples but was still without generalizations people could use. I needed a better conceptualization of *the link between an act and its subsequent effect on the mind.*

A further discovery helped illuminate the search. It had to do with people's sense of how *feasible* their alternative is when they act. A rule seemed almost universal. It is this: A person who does something while sensing the presence of some feasible alternative influences himself more than if there seemed no feasible alternative. The acts that seem to permit alternatives affect us most.

I was working with a novelist who had written a successful book but whose last two books were not successes. He had stopped writing and felt broken. I knew enough to realize that if he tried again, returning to his room and concentrating, it would be of some value to his spirits. He had rented a loft for the purpose and was starting to go there to work. It seemed vital to him that he do his writing away from home. He wavered, going there every day for weeks and feeling optimistic about his future, but then hiding away at home, not answering the phone and not even thinking about writing. He knew this flight was damaging to his spirit, but at those times it didn't seem to matter.

During one period, heavy snow fell and his car was stuck in the garage. He might stay home and then argue vehemently with me that there was nothing he could do—his papers were all in the loft. However, his brother telephoned him with an offer to lend him a car. He refused, and that refusal made an enormous difference.

Now his choice to stay home took on an utterly different meaning from the one it would have had. He was responding to what he sensed had been a real option. He felt less capable, less likely to finish a book at all, and more pessimistic about his future. Although he hid his brother's offer from me for a time, *he knew* it had been made. The real issue was not what I thought, but how his behavior affected him. Because he renounced an alternative he felt was feasible, his behavior exerted a different impact on him than if there were really nothing else he could do.

People sense the feasibility of alternatives when they act. With this knowledge, I could frequently tell when people were rationalizing. Whatever excuses they made to themselves to extenuate an act, these did not affect their own reaction to what they had done. If in fact they were telling the truth, that an alternative seemed utterly out of the question, then their choice would not have an appreciable effect on their mental state. But if they were rationalizing, it would have.

Time and again I could see that the choices affecting people most were *those they felt offered real alternatives.*

Each of us has a frontier of feasible alternatives, and we respond to our own acts to some extent as if grading ourselves, using this frontier as our standard. As we accomplish more, our sense of what is feasible becomes modified. To my surprise I discovered that even people who seem to have little sense of their capacities were continually responding to ideas about what was feasible for them.

I was starting to make inferences about how people felt by watching how their behavior affected them. I could tell whether they felt they had acted with real options. Sometimes I could even tell when a new option came into a person's life or went out of it, though the person had not re-

ported it to me. The effect on them of their having that
option became evident.

For instance, a woman is no longer in love with her
husband but stays reasonably satisfied with him while her
children are young. There seems no real option to leave.
Gradually, she starts to lose confidence, to hate herself and
him, although the only real change in her life is that the
children are in school and she has gotten a good-paying job.
After some years of having a real option to leave but staying
because she is afraid she can't live alone or meet someone
else, she despises herself.

As people told me about decisions they made, I could
often tell that they secretly felt they might preferably have
acted in some other way. They didn't always admit this, and
might hardly know it. But something in their present vision
of existence told me that they'd renounced some alternative.

The role of the feasible alternative helped explain why
my prevailing on patients to act in particular ways had
sometimes actually *detracted* from the value of their acting.
Certain acts, such as trusting people or asserting oneself,
might have helped the patient ordinarily. But if I became
too vehement, the patient would act with the feeling that
otherwise I might withdraw my loyalty. It would seem to
the patient that there was little real alternative. It was do
the thing or lose my support. That was not literally so, but
many patients were accustomed to having parents who with-
drew from them when they were not well behaved. They
carried that expectation with them and applied it to me.
Since they acted without a sense of possessing a feasible
alternative, acts that might otherwise have been beneficial
were of little or no value to them.

That people possess a sense of what they can feasibly do
has vital implications that I did not see until much later. It
accounted for the potential that even severely handicapped
people always retain for self-satisfaction and happiness. Many
such people seem at peace with conditions far worse than
would be tolerable to the rest of us. Even those severely

handicapped respond more than it seems to what they have been making of their current lives. Their standards reflect what they sense is currently feasible for them to do. There is thus a stunning form of democracy built into the human psyche—one that affords perpetual possibilities. Highly accomplished people cannot be assured of a durable sense of well-being, and those of us defeated in the past always retain the possibility of redemption.

At this point I felt utterly sure that many acts, if not all, influence a person's psyche. Also that rewards bear a subtler relationship to an activity than merely stimulating it, and that the feasibility of an alternative is relevant to the impact that an act will produce. I could see a connection between the last two ideas. Once the secretary was offered a huge reward for extra work, she no longer had the easy alternative of going home. It was important that she renounce a feasible alternative for her helping the boss to be of the benefit that it might be. She herself had sensed the preferability of acting without the additional incentive, the importance so far as her own self-esteem and outlook were concerned. Rewards, in diminishing the feasibility of an alternative, often deprive an act of its value to the person in just such a way.

I found it encouraging to see how much we respond to our acts in the recent past. To that extent, we are not helpless victims of our own histories. Still, I was very unclear as to the laws by which we could predict in advance how particular decisions were to affect us. What would we have to know in advance to make such judgments?

At least the nature of the search was becoming clear. I had a keener sense of what I was after: laws, as nearly universal as possible, that people use to determine the effect on them exerted by their own choices.

CHAPTER SEVEN

What Guilt Teaches Us

The study of guilt isolates beautifully certain ways our acts affect the mind. My next theoretical advance came from this study. The inevitability of consequence seems manifest. The person who violates a code and then feels guilty can testify to the virtual impossibility of avoiding the guilt after the act has been committed. And here we see an interesting twist. Continued violation of one's personal ethic *reduces* guilt over the activity. The very behavior that originally produces the guilt seems to have the opposite effect after a while.

I began to study instances in which people eradicated their guilt by repeating the very activity that evoked the feeling. The more I studied them, the more I saw that such erasure of guilt by actions is the rule rather than the exception. In particular, these examples taught me to make a distinction that has wide applicability, distinction between the way an act *feels on the spot* and the *actual effect on the psyche*. My first true awareness of this distinction came from investigating my own guilt and its fluctuations in response to my own behavior.

During months when I was well disciplined about my writing, I observed that I felt unmistakably guilty after a day of not working when I might have. On the days there had been opportunity to work and I had not, I felt myself a failure. Sometimes there were several such days in a row. The feeling of letting myself down was keen. Sometimes the guilt became a sensory experience. A community of readers seemed to be waiting for my next book, and I was disappointing them. I could almost hear them murmuring that I was not the wonder I had pretended to be. Such a community was, of course, my own invention. The people in it were personifications of the demand for my highest ideal—my conscience. In working for them, I was working for myself. I accepted the grandiosity of my own view as useful, since without offending anyone it made me feel at the center of the universe and added importance to my life. Such guilt, whether or not it included this vision, was valuable. It spurred me on to make up the lost time. And I treasured my guilty conscience as more than a spur. It was a curious kind of comfort.

When the run of days during which I was delinquent extended beyond a certain point, I could sense that the guilt lessened. After one long avoidant period, I could hardly hear their voices. It was as if I had run so far away from home that I could no longer hear the community beseeching me to come back, to do something important with my life. A different *worldview* created by my defaults was replacing the sharp sense of obligation and optimism that had kept me at attention. There was no community murmuring about my failure. The target had receded too. I recalled Browning's line about "the need of a world for men like me." The sense that there was such a world and such a need meant every- thing, and I was in the process of destroying it.

I saw the same phenomenon in other people—in certain painters and sculptors and writers, for example, who were patients of mine. As they fled from their efforts, they at first felt guilt but, by avoidance over a long period, tended to dim their guilt along with their dreams of accomplishment. I later saw that the same held for criminals. The first crime, the first break with any tradition one has upheld, is tinged with fear and guilt. It feels as if all human history were watching, startled at the new behavior. But repetition dulls conscience and the vision that accompanies it. This was evidently an important instance in which choices exerted an effect on one's mental state—an effect that was easy to see in accumulation.

When counseling juvenile offenders, my aim was to encourage them to contribute something to society, or at least to prepare themselves to do so. It was important that they try long enough to convince themselves that they had something to offer. In the process they would restore a sense of guilt so that trying would feel more reasonable to them.

A comparison of two quotations illustrates the kind of change that occurs. The first is taken from the testimony of a criminal, given after his first crime:

> Another night four of us went searching for a drunken man, and we ran across an old man with snow white hair who was drunk. . . . The fellow that was supposed to put the arm on him didn't have the heart to do it. . . . We went through his pockets, and got about twenty-one dollars. We left a five-dollar bill in his pocket and never touched the packages that he was carrying. We none of us ever bragged about this brave thing that we had done. . . . I had a strong presentiment of danger that night and I didn't want to sleep at the club. I guess it was because I knew that I deserved anything that might happen to me.[52]

Compare this with the attitude of a hardened criminal, fictitious this time though commonplace in real life, as described by Mark Twain:

> [Pudd'nhead Wilson's act] preyed upon his rag of a con-

science; but after that he began to get comfortable again, and was presently able to sleep like any other miscreant.

Repetition of a crime gradually tears down one's belief in the old standards and the act ceases to feel criminal. The problem faced by most criminals is not that their behavior continues to plague them. It is that what they do repeatedly comes to seem right—or at least becomes a matter of relative indifference. With their decline of conscience goes the loss of the community they once imagined. There are occasional exceptions that I was able to explain later on, but invariably the hardened criminal has been hardened by his own behavior over an extended period of time.

This was the first hint I had that what we commonly call conscience is not a fixed part of us. It does not become implanted in childhood at some crucial stage. Rather, our conscience is sustained by our choices. It was, as I thought about it, as if a great superstructure, which had seemed as constant as the mountains surrounding a village, were beginning to melt. One had to wonder how many other seemingly deep-rooted aspects of our psychic lives would yield to change if particular actions were taken.

It was startling to consider that even the very first violation of a standard, while it causes the pain of remorse, also has the unseen effect of whittling down the standard just a little. So does each successive violation. After a while the guilt becomes less, because the internalized standard is less stringent. It was this study of guilt, my own and other people's, that gave me my first clear sense that a single act may exert two simultaneous but highly different kinds of effects on a person. The more important effect isn't the emotion that the person actually experiences; it is the imperceptible shift in outlook—in the way the person views himself and others, and in the values that are part of this perception. With each act, the person is rearranging his own mental state slightly so that similar acts seem more rational, even routine, in the future.

I had as yet no systematic way of knowing what the effects on the mental state were going to be. Still, it was exciting to realize that small as they were, they were there, and that they *accumulated*. That gave them importance. They remained in the mind and were additive—like deposits in a bank. Emotions, though keenly felt, are *transitory*—like the pain that accompanies sacrifice when money is saved, or the pleasure in spending it.

I thought about the distinction applied in the cases I had studied. The woman who by acts of trust softened her expectations of men had done something that was difficult for her. But her distress when she took a chance was only temporary. On the other hand, the slight rearrangement of mental state that she produced was a real and durable change. So was the change of outlook that the 57-year-old man produced by forcing himself to apply for jobs despite his misgivings.

Recognizing these more durable effects became my task. It would no longer suffice to observe how people felt when they acted. What mattered were the microscopic changes of mental state that their acts produced. My direction was becoming clearer. It was to study the relationship between voluntary acts and such effects. These effects on the mental state were inevitable consequences of choices; I had to assume they followed definite laws. Knowing those laws would enable one to make choices with inner change in mind.

Not long afterward I came upon a whole group of people who differentiated between these accumulative effects on the mental state and one's personal experiences while acting. They were drug counselors, whom I was training in methods of therapy at a rehabilitation center. They didn't reflect on the generality of the distinction they were drawing. But they made it regularly and where it counted most with the addicts they tried to help. Being former addicts themselves, they knew the problem well. What's good feels awful, and what's awful feels good. Moreover, they understood that there was a real gain produced by each decision of the addict to refrain.

They recognized that some shift of outlook was occurring, and that benefits could be accumulated. They knew that as addicts went on refraining, enduring the agony for a long time, a change would occur. The addict would feel more like doing other things associated with a better life. Eventually, the value of all that suffering would be seen—as if enough gossamer had been gathered and now the faint tapestry of a new existence could be truly seen for the first time.

Breaking lesser habits, too, is often seen to have implications for the rest of life. The smoker who quits is likely to become more optimistic generally, even more health conscious, and to enjoy still other benefits. Especially at the start, even in these most successful cases the person experiences torment and a sense of deprivation. But, as we have seen, feelings themselves are not additive. Because he is gradually altering his underlying mental state, the time will come when as an ex-smoker he will feel *less* deprived than he did.

The trouble was, I found, that these crucial effects could be identified only in retrospect, if at all. They could be appreciated only after many instances of the same kind of change had been accumulated by repetition of the same behavior. At that stage of my work, if I wanted to make predictions, they would have to be based on the experiences reported by other people who broke similar habits. An occasional exception would occur if I detected some slight change due to behavior recently begun. I could speculate that more of the same activity would engrain the change and probably enlarge it, and I was usually right.

People would need a method of determining the impact on their mental state; the impact not just of breaking habits, but of *any* particular choice. Ultimately, I needed a generalization applying to all individual acts. How could a person foretell the effects of any decision under consideration?

CHAPTER EIGHT
The "Habit Criterion"

In a handful of cases, there was a way of anticipating what effects a certain act would have, even though the act was not part of any habit. One could *think* of it as part of a habit. If I could infer how repetition of the same act would affect the person's mental state, I could use the knowledge to conclude that the single act was doing the same. The difference would be only in degree. No matter that these microscopic changes caused by the single act could not be seen individually. Use of what I called the *habit criterion* would, if I was right, enable me to infer the nature of these changes —and even to foretell them.

The question to ask, then, was: *Suppose the person made a habit of such acts. How would that habit affect his mental state?* Whatever the answer, his doing the thing even once was going to affect him in precisely the same way.

Naturally, I couldn't always foretell what the impact of such a sequence would be. But there were also cases in which I felt I could surmise it reasonably well from past experience.

I remember one of the earliest times I predicted to a

patient in detail how a single act would affect his outlook on life. What I said relied almost completely on the use of the habit criterion. I was treating a boy who was in the process of deciding whether to commit a robbery along with several friends. The boy respected his mother, a scrupulous and hard-working woman who was divorced and who had brought him up alone. But his belief in his ability to do well in college and his evaluation of what it could do for him were uncertain. He condescended to come to my office and discuss his plans. We agreed at once that his mother often misunderstood him. But crime was another story.

While I was talking with him, there flashed through my mind the picture of what repeated crimes would most likely do to his outlook. After making a habit of crime, almost surely he would feel even less capable of going to college. He would doubt his capacity more. A certain kind of hardness and remoteness would come over him. He would feel less worthy of the love of worthwhile women and would feel more generally estranged. To my delight, he agreed with these predictions. But then he made the obvious argument that he was not contemplating a life of crime.

But, I assured him, the single act of robbing the clothing store together with his friends would initiate such a shift in his outlook. Such emotions as the excitement of the doing, and perhaps the remorse or pride afterwards, would fill his mind. He might become preoccupied with a flood of other thoughts, such as what to do with the stolen property and whom to tell, if anyone. The really important shift in outlook would not be perceptible. But it would occur, assuredly, in exactly the same way that a life of crime would ultimately cause it to change. Perhaps the only early symptoms would be a slightly lowered respect for his mother and greater difficulty in doing his homework. But the shift would be real, I repeated. Perhaps because he liked me, he took my word for it. In any event, I prevailed—or rather, his choice not to commit the crime prevailed.

Had I rested my case against his committing a crime on

the usual moral arguments, I probably would have gotten nowhere. I would have sounded just like his mother, who had made him sick of moral arguments by using them against sex, against staying out late, as well as against consorting with certain boys who were known delinquents. The other argument, that crime does not pay because one is likely to get caught, might have influenced him in exactly the opposite way from what I hoped for. How could I be so sure? Why did I doubt his ability to pull the perfect crime? No. It had been necessary to grant the truth, that in all likelihood he could steal at least once and get away with it. He was becoming an adult, with an adult's ability to think and plan. But the effect of the act on him was inevitable and inescapable. He wouldn't be able to avoid that. I found a stronger argument against his committing a crime than that of morality or risk. And though I certainly could not foretell the special effect of every act and predict it for the person, I became able to use this newfound knowledge in a way that was satisfying both to the person involved and to myself.

After thinking about it, I gained further insight into why my analysis was right. The emotions that originally accompany an act tend to diminish as the act becomes habitual. As an act becomes routine, it gradually ceases to evoke such reactions as delight or remorse, or any of the feelings that it brought when it was novel. Thus the impact of the whole habit is composed of the *durable* imprint, the kind of imprint I was interested in—and not at all of transitory reactions. Studying the habit isolated the secret but significant change in the psyche produced by the single choice.

The same method could be applied in certain other cases I had already studied. I could easily imagine the habit of avoiding job interviews because one feels old; the habit of agreeing with people in authority; the habit of jogging and dieting to stay in good health. It wasn't hard to envision at least certain of the effects that such behavior would produce. The person in each instance would undergo a mental accommodation to his routine behavior. He would feel old and unworthy of jobs; he would feel unentitled to disagree with those in authority and uncertain of his own opinions; he would develop a belief in the importance of good physical condition. The impact observable after such repetition would, in a smaller degree, be the effect of even a single decision of the particular kind. Every instance of fearful agreement with those in authority would undermine the person's belief in himself. Forcing oneself to do a program of exercises even once would do a little to build one's belief in the importance of continuing such a program. These results would occur, though unseen and perhaps clouded by other reactions that the person might experience at the time.

The habit criterion furnishes logical proof that every act, and not just certain ones, affects the mental state. Every act either belongs to a habit or doesn't. Suppose the act belongs to a habit. As part of the habit it affects the mental state, since every act in the chain contributes. We know this because if the person acted otherwise, the habit would be slower to form and the state of mind would not be acquired so soon.

The proof holds even if the act is not followed up. Reason this way. Were the act followed up, and a habit based on such acts, then the effect of the act would be seen as that of the habit. It would be the first act of the habit. The act inaugurating a habit exerts an effect on the mind that is the same as that of the whole habit. Therefore, the act in this case, too, must be affecting the mental state. If it does not receive the support of similar actions, this means only that its contribution gets washed away later, which in no way contradicts the fact that the contribution was made. Therefore, every act exerts an influence on the mental state, whether or not subsequent behavior of the same kind makes it inferable.

For a time, the habit criterion looked like a huge magnifying glass that could enlarge the unseen impact of a single choice, thereby making it visible. As a theoretical tool it was invaluable, establishing beyond doubt that all choices exert imperceptible effects on the mental state. The criterion, however, had only limited practical use. In some cases, a long-run repetition seemed so unlikely that to talk about it was almost preposterous. My insights might have been right, but they certainly weren't persuasive. One patient laughed outright at such an interpretation.

A woman whose close friend had stolen away her lover decided to sever her relationship with both friend and lover abruptly. But two months later, because she remained occasionally bothered by thoughts of the two of them together, she plotted revenge. She would give a huge party for the purpose of not inviting this other woman. Word would surely get back to her, and the woman would suffer when she heard what she had missed.

My patient felt uplifted by the contemplation of her revenge. But by applying the habit criterion to the act, I could see at once the harm it would do. Suppose she made a regular practice of giving such parties? Even assuming she could afford them and that guests would come, how would this regular practice affect her? It would keep her feeling obsessed by the other woman. It would keep her mindful of what the other woman had done and would renew a sense of hopelessness. It might make the other woman the most important person in her life. It would center her whole outlook on the need to avenge this terrible misdeed.

The single act—of giving the party for revenge—would do all this, only to a lesser degree. None of these effects on her thinking would be easily traceable to the single choice. And yet that choice would rearrange her outlook for the worse in just those ways. The habit criterion implied that such a result would occur.

The conclusion did not seem to me far-fetched—to evaluate an act of revenge by reference to a conjured-up long-term habit of revenge. Such an act makes the victim and his crime seem more important, just as a habit of revenge would evidently do.

I recalled reading a startling assertion made in 1917 by an anthropologist, R. Rivers, that certain tribes keep alive their thirst for revenge by taking revenge.[6] Other anthropologists had been preoccupied with looking for the roots of the desire for revenge without appreciating that the very behavior might be replenishing it. Rivers had noted a particular case in which people sustain an outlook by an ongoing activity, the phenomenon I was engaged in studying.

When I told my patient that she would poison herself with thoughts about her enemy, she took me quite seriously. She seemed concerned. However, when I told her how I knew, explaining the habit criterion and how it applied, she laughed. It was indeed preposterous to imagine herself, or anyone, giving a sequence of revenge parties. The habit criterion, though it pinpointed the unseen effect of the single choice, simply wasn't convincing to her. And I met the same problem with other people.

In still other cases, I was unable to picture what the outcome of the long-term habit would be. The method relied too heavily on conjecture. Too often the long-run behavior was fictitious, nothing more than a speculation made for the purpose of understanding the single act. And the conceptualization had little more to recommend it than a guess about the act itself. The method worked best when the activity was one that others had engaged in at length and that almost always affected them similarly. It also worked when the person was already, very evidently, making a habit of the behavior in question, and I could discern some of its long-term effects. It did not succeed when the act was novel, when there seemed no reasonable way of picturing its repetition or inferring what the long-term effect of such repetition would be.

Unless I could learn more, talking about habits instead of individual acts looked like a dead end. The habit criterion would remain a mere philosophy akin to "Act as you would want others to act" or "Act as if each day were your last on earth." Though perhaps sound advice, these suggestions teach nothing about how to evaluate the desirability of particular behavior.

What I needed next was a reliable way of knowing what *habits* do to the mind. From there, it would be a short step to discovering the same about individual choices.

CHAPTER NINE

The Impact of Habits

How do our habits affect the mind? I devoted myself to observing and recording changes occurring in people as they acquire habits. It promised to be easier to compile a catalog of this kind than one of the impact of individual acts. While collecting entries, I observed that, more than I'd thought, people tend to repeat what they do. What I had taken to be the impact of a choice was not so in some cases, but rather, was the impact of a whole habit of which the single choice was only a component.

My research into what others said about habits showed that the different schools of psychology each approached habits in their characteristic ways. Frontier psychology had taken a deep interest in how habits are formed, and what they accomplish. James had been influenced in his approach to habits by two British philosophers, John Stuart Mill and Alexander Bain. Mill had stressed the importance of habits in putting forth his notion of character as a "completely fashioned will," and Bain had actually talked about the ability of moral behavior to "accumulate moral forces in the mind." James embraced these two ideas and emphasized the role that good habits can play in making the person's "nervous system an ally." However, as when studying single acts, they stopped short of considering the person's subjective state, as if it were the activity alone that mattered. Their dictum, often expressed, was, "Do it no matter why." They sometimes even imagined that if a person did a thing for the wrong reasons, he would profit more.

Meanwhile, nineteenth-century novelists, playwrights, and philosophers were cultivating a profound appetite for learning about these inner states. Then came psychoanalysis. But while conveying the importance of inner states, psychoanalysis downgrades the significance of habits, as it does that of individual acts so far as their impact on the mind is concerned. In regarding underlying states as the only true causes of behavior, it disputes that control over habits can be determinative. By overlooking that habitual choices might themselves recharge the mind, it has added virtually nothing to our knowledge of what habits actually do to us psychologically.

To behaviorism, that habits exist at all is a source of embarrassment. It is essential to modern behaviorist theory to maintain that nonreinforced behavior stops. But the very nature of a habit is in the fact that the person continues to do the thing, even if the act goes unrewarded. Habits would appear to constitute a class of acts that do not need the usual outside reinforcement.

Behaviorists could not study the ways in which habitual choices affect the mind for numerous reasons. First, they do not believe that nonreinforced behavior persists. Second, they do not think of the acts constituting a habit as the causal agents. Finally, they have scant (if any) interest in subjective experience. As far back as 1932 the behaviorist Knight Dunlap denied that an act ever makes itself more likely. In his book on habits, Dunlap, when differentiating between a good habit and a bad one, does not include the distinction that certain habits have beneficial effects on the mind and others do not.

There have, however, been several voices in the wilderness in the 1940s and 1950s, psychologists who believed that *doing* a thing affects the mind critically, that the act makes the difference.

The first, Edwin Guthrie, had a sizable following for a while. His essential idea was that "if you do something in a given situation, the next time you are in that situation you will tend to do the same thing again." Simple as this sounds at first, its implications were startling. He was saying that you will *always* repeat yourself if conditions are the same. He denied that reinforcements are ever in themselves determinative of how people act.

But we see that people and lower animals tend to repeat the things that bring them advantages. Guthrie explained this by arguing that even where reinforcements are given—such as food given to a caged animal for pressing the right lever—the reinforcement itself does not essentially account for the learning. The reinforcement changes the animal's situation. It terminates the phase of looking for a solution. Next time, when returned to a similar situation, the animal —*because of the way it acted, not essentially because of the reinforcement*—is more likely to act that way again. It will do what it did *last*. This tendency to repeat behavior, he believed, is built into the physiology of man and lower animals. That reinforcements such as food terminate the exploratory sequence is what gives them their importance to learning.

Guthrie thus believed that what an animal does has the crucial effect upon it. The act sets some mechanism within the creature, human or beast, and predisposes it to do the same thing again. He believed that acts affect the organism.

From Guthrie came encouragement. His was truly an original theory of learning. He conceived that the way the organism's own behavior affects it is worth studying as a cause. Guthrie, however, would talk only about what was measurable, which meant he did not consider people's subjective states. For him, the elements that counted were all physical—the animal's bodily state, its bodily posture when acting, and the stimuli brought to bear upon it just before acting.

From my point of view, it was not something about a person's bodily posture that I needed to know, but something more about people's inner lives, if I were to understand more precisely how their acts affected them.

The other psychologist on the right track for me was Gordon Allport. He too presented the idea that behavior influences the mind apart from whether it is reinforced. Allport was highly esteemed academically and widely read publicly. His theories about habits were hotly debated. Allport believed that some behavior, though not all, is "functionally autonomous": the behavior goes on by itself. The activity produces the drive for subsequent behavior of the same kind. Allport's term "functional autonomy" does not emphasize a person's control over the process; it even suggests that the whole process is out of his hands. Still, the activity is doing something—it is to that extent conceptualized as a cause, even if the activity too is determined.

Allport was ready to talk about people's inner lives, their motives. He disagreed with the Freudian view that old motives continue to operate, arguing that all motives are contemporary.

For instance, Allport described a young man who studied hard to impress adults. Over the years he found a field that fascinated him; he became a researcher, still working hard but without any of his original motivation. For a psychoanalyst to describe him as still trying to please his father would be to attribute a past motive to his current behavior and would be wrong, argued Allport. Such past motives are truly gone. They do not continue to reside in the unconscious and motivate our daily acts but are completely replaced by contemporary ones.

This view sounds simple enough. Yet many of us harbor

a sense that we have not truly escaped the past, that somehow early motives still haunt us—even though we have also acquired adult, contemporary motives for our behavior. My investigations were to reveal some stunning corroboration that their traces often remain, and to explain why.

Habit smooths out performance. The person acquiring a habit acts with a definite intention. In forming the habit, the person tends to drop waste motions out of the activity and at the same time tends to lose touch with his original reason for the activity—all as part of the economy of habits. Sometimes the person can easily summon up his real reason for the activity, but often not. For instance, a bartender at first puts his hand on the bar to show he is relaxed and to indicate he is listening to his customers when his mind is really elsewhere. It is a decoy that works. Now on busy nights as he hurries down the length of the bar, his hand brushes over it. He has no thought of conveying a message to anyone, but the message is sent.

The person, after reaching his conclusion about how to act in some situation, is thus able to repeat his solution automatically, without having to think about the problem each time. One can see the survival value in this. The person does the thing faster, more accurately, with less effort, and sometimes without any thought, once the habit has been formed. Habits free consciousness so that the person can devote his higher mental faculties to new challenges.

I was doing my best to identify the impact of individual habits. One way was to compare people's outlook during periods when they engaged in the habit most and when they least engaged in it. Rarely, however, could I feel very confident of a cause-and-effect relationship. By this time, I had influenced a few colleagues and therapists whom I was training, and some helped me greatly by watching for such changes and reporting them. They were used to asking, What does the habit reveal? and I was introducing the subject of how the habit affects the person.

Then I realized that I was much better positioned to see the effects on the mind of *breaking* a habit than those of forming one. People seldom knew they were about to form a habit. It was hard to know where to look. By contrast, they knew in advance much more often that they intended to break some habit if they could, and while doing so they would readily report their reactions. Studying the decomposition of habits became my main method—analysis by postmortem. I would compare a patient's outlook before attacking the habit and after he had successfully broken it—that is, freed himself, for all practical purposes, of the urge for the activity.

While watching, I sometimes marveled at the differences in what breaking a habit meant to people. Take the activity of smoking cigarettes. I had a number of patients who quit smoking and who reported only an occasional and easily controllable urge to smoke a year or so later. They had that in common. But under closer scrutiny, I could see that the actual effects on their mental state were quite different. Some felt sudden new awareness of health as they succeeded. A few felt more concerned about their budget and were heartened in frugality by their victory over the cost of cigarettes. There were unmistakable differences in what the same activity meant to these people, as evidenced by their reaction to its removal. How could a person know the effect that breaking a habit was to have? I remembered the description by James of the "intensely active gap" one feels when a conclusion is almost in sight.

All along I had observed that habits come in *clusters*; individual habits seem connected with others. This had only vague meaning to me, though I had different ways of knowing it. I had seen that people have sets of habits that they tend to indulge at the same time. For instance, a man would habitually accuse people of mistakes. Almost before he knew it, he would tell even sensitive people they'd let him down, and then he would feel sorry. He was too quick to explain away his own mistakes. He also had the habits of raising his voice and gesticulating with his hands when he talked. His gestures were comical, and he was constantly told to talk lower. In certain periods of life he would do all these things much more than at others. I could tell from his tone on the telephone how much he was gesticulating, and whether he was in the vein to blame people. His activities rose and fell in consonance. As if they shared some impulse.

Related was the observation of a phenomenon that has been much debated in psychological literature, that of *replacement*. When a person is stymied acting in one habitual way, he tends to substitute other behavior to satisfy the same want—to *replace* the missing habit. When a person fights one habit, his urge for the other increases. The idea originally comes from psychoanalysis: That people tend to replace habitual behavior was one of Freud's discoveries. He construed it as meaning that powerful, underlying motives govern behavior, and that there is no sense in trying to combat them. One will only end up by replacing the activity, probably with a worse one. Freud took replacement as signifying that behavior is truly symptomatic of motive and nothing more. His description of it as "symptom substitution" has already been mentioned. Implicit was his idea that there is a powerful inner life that motivates behavior and will not be denied its expression, and the idea that changes of behavior can have no real effect on the inner life.

Behaviorists took issue. But the disposition to substitute one particular activity for another has actually come to the attention of behaviorists. Recall the experiment by Goldiamond, who treated a man for shouting at his wife. Goldiamond observed along the way that

> since in the absence of yelling at his wife the subject sulked and since the program was designed to reduce yelling, the subject's sulking was in danger of increasing.

Indeed, we can hardly force ourselves to break a habit, certainly not one that matters, without looking for a replacement. Often there are obvious ones. But what in particular linked sulking and yelling? Why more sulking when the yelling was cut down?

The switch to a replacement could be made in fantasy. I would ask a person what he felt like doing at the time of giving up a habit. Nearly always, when the impulse for the renounced activity was high, there would also be an urge to engage in particular other activities. Members of the cluster that rose and fell together also tended to substitute for one another. That is, if stymied in carrying out one activity, the person would tend to substitute another, or several others, from the same cluster. The common denominator of habits comprising a cluster is their *motive*. Activities within a cluster are all aimed at accomplishing the same end.

In the case of the man whose voice got too loud and who gesticulated to the extent of looking like a comic strip character, by these activities he was saying, "Please pay attention to me. See me. Don't discount me or abandon me." The same motive underlay his telling other people that they misunderstood him or harmed him. And he expressed it also in his constant defense of himself when none was called for. He felt in danger of being utterly disregarded, and he would battle for appreciation, virtually accusing people of denying it to him. Not only did these habits rise and fall in consonance; when the man was stymied in the expression of one of them he would feel the impulse to express the same need by another activity from the set. He was expressing the same motive, which, loosely speaking, we can call his "aggressive defensiveness."

What would happen if the man systematically fought to discontinue all those behaviors at once, treated them as comprising one grand pattern, and tried to starve himself of whatever satisfaction such behavior had afforded him? The answer was that with an all-out attack on the behavior, often the person *could actually do away with the motive* after a time.

I saw the same later with hundreds of people, especially

after I'd become more adept at helping them identify real clusters. There would be an initial crisis, even more acute than when someone refrained from a single habit. The underlying motivation would rise up repeatedly and become enormous—the backwash of trying to break the whole cluster of habits. During this period of terrible temptation, it took special caution not to try to replace one activity by another springing from the same unwanted motive. But as the person continued to resist such a cluster, its core motivation would soon decline. With my help, many people could grasp the method, spot some harmful motivation—such as the desire to ingratiate themselves—identify various related ways they did this, and stop them. In very many cases, their motivation, after rising initially, diminished. They did away with the motive or greatly reduced it.

I could see why the method had not been tried by people on their own. Without the logic guiding such a resolution, a person would be unlikely to deprive himself this way, of expressing a motive, even for a short time. Wanting some unavailable activity, the person would, as a rule, automatically try to replace it by another satisfying much of, if not all, the same need. The motivation would thus receive nourishment from a new source and seem ingrained and without any dependency at all on the person's behavior.

That every act renews its motivation accounted for a startling number of my previous formulations. Indeed, I could now see that many of these formulations were only instances of this rule. In recognizing the significance to people of whether they felt they had a feasible alternative when acting, I realized that what I'd been observing was the role of their motivation. If there seemed a feasible alternative, then in declining a challenge, people would undermine their confidence. If there seemed none, retreat would not be the same act of cowardice and would not have the same effect on their outlook. The significance of the person's subjective state when acting was becoming clear. I'd been right in realizing that it was the person's impression about alternatives, rather than the actuality, that counted.

The role of rewards also derived from their influence on the person's motive. With a huge reward the person is likely to switch his motive from what it was to a straightforward desire for the reward. The activity then renews this desire mainly, and the effort loses its former value. I could also see why it mattered so much whether a patient did something primarily to please me or to benefit himself. With the motive of pleasing me, he would merely reinstate that motive, inject it more into the mainstream of his thinking. He would not produce independence or self-esteem.

Something even more startling was happening. As the person's motive changed, so did the relevant perceptions. I began to realize that in his stopping the behavior, he was doing more than to alter a motive. As the motive lost strength, a concomitant change took place in the person's whole vision of existence—usually in his appraisal of himself and his picture of other people. The person, in reducing the motive, was teaching himself to perceive and feel differently.

Take the man I mentioned who constantly accused people of making mistakes, of letting him down, who denied his own faults, and who did nearly anything he could to center attention on himself. At the core of his constant desire to retain a spotless reputation, never to be found in the wrong, was a picture of himself that might be approximated this way: I'm a barely adequate person in a competitive world. People are on the verge of disqualifying me and might do so if they caught me in one mistake. There is little room for me, but perhaps I can salvage something by guarding my reputation vigilantly and giving people no pretext for rejecting me.

This was the very way of perceiving that changed when he stopped the cluster of activities. His stopping did more than reduce the impulses. It altered his whole way of perceiving himself and others. He felt less in error throughout the day, and less on the brink of being unmasked and disqualified.

Time and again, I could see that a person's activities were sending to the mind some picture of existence, the very view that would change if the person stopped those activities. The collection of activities was sending a message to the mind: I am a certain kind of person in a certain kind of world, and I had better do this to get what I want. Discontinuing even one activity, if the person didn't replace it with others having the same motive, would invariably alter the picture.

It was as if each activity contributed its own information to the total outlook, the person's full mental state. Sometimes the change seemed mainly in the person's perception of himself: sometimes it centered almost entirely in his vision of others. Always it involved both, and much more.

I conceptualized this vision of life associated with an activity as a *worldview*, in the German sense of *Weltanschauung*. It has implicit in it a whole philosophy of life. And it is also specific in its imagery. This worldview, this glimpse of reality, has ideas concerning a person's worth to others and his expectations of how they will treat him, and an idea as to whether it is deserved.

Each cluster of habits was sending a worldview to the mind, the one connected with the habits in that cluster. Studying the cluster had been for me a way of enlarging the effects of the individual habits, and so I could conjecture that the individual habits were each sending that worldview upward, reconvincing the person of it. And the habit itself exerted only the effect that the individual choices, its components, had introduced individually. The habit criterion teaches us that the meaning of the act is equivalent to that of the habit.

My reasoning led to a stunning conclusion. Although one could not measure separately the inner effects of individual choices, a remarkable and highly useful statement could be made about them. Behind every choice there is a worldview —extremely complex and at best able to be articulated only in part. Competing worldviews lie behind possible alternatives that a person can choose. The choice actually made, whatever its impact on his external situation, has the immediate effect of sending a message to the mind. It tells the person that its particular worldview is justified, correct.

Of course, if the person perceives some ill effect of the act, he may make a new decision. A person has this much pliancy. He may decide never to do the thing again. But when the person is acting habitually, unthinkingly, as we all must most of the time, his ongoing activities are fortifying the complex worldview he already holds.

The idea seemed elusive and yet incredibly simple. Every voluntary act produces a slight readjustment in the mind toward that act. *The mind accepts somewhat the reason for the act.* This means we must always choose between worldviews that we already entertain. A person without generosity or confidence cannot suddenly adopt these feelings as traits. But among the possible worldviews that go through the mind, anyone's mind, are alternatives, some nearer the desired direction than others. It doesn't make sense to simply act like the person one wants to be, because the worldview behind such a choice would be pretense or wishful thinking. However, taking one step at a time, one can make choices designed to cultivate qualities—for instance, to overcome fear and make generosity possible, and to create confidence, along with the mode of perception that goes with confidence.

Spelled out, a good approximation of the discovery might be this. There are different worldviews connected with alternative possibilities of behaving that come to a person's mind. A choice is an election of one worldview over the others. Every choice reinforces its motivating worldview, predisposes the person to see life through the lens of it. We might think of habits as so many tubes of color that, when pressed, add their tint to the person's total perception. Indeed, every decision does this somewhat.

Later, I was to add this refinement. If there are various motives, then the convictions behind them are renewed in proportion to their contribution as motives for that act. Moreover, the worldview behind alternatives actually renounced is dimmed, also in proportion to how feasible they felt at the time.

The principle itself has never ceased to be exciting to me, in its many variations. Simple as it sounds, it is important as a theoretical underpinning, as a way of understanding the impact of habits and of strategies that one can design to take pliancy into one's own hands. There is, of course, a great deal still to be learned. But the impact exerted on the mind by individual acts seems established in this principle.

Often a person can recognize the worldview that underlies a contemplated decision. With this knowledge, one can put the principle into action. A man argues, "The boss won't give me the raise I deserve for my honesty and hard work. From now on I'll pad my expense account as some other employees are doing. It's a dog-eat-dog world, and you have to do that." His earlier efforts had sustained his belief that hard work is usually rewarded, and his hope that it would be rewarded in his case. There was also a keen belief that it *ought* to be rewarded—a sense not truly dependent on the real facts. His contemplated behavior will unconvince him of this. It will seem more than ever a world in which honesty isn't rewarded, and isn't its own reward. What now seems like unfairness will soon seem less so; it will be taken more naturally as the way of the world. Such changes, in one's sense of what ought to be, infallibly mirror people's loss of optimism. Perhaps it would be better to leave the job altogether, to take a demotion or learn some new skill than to succumb and suffer this corrosion. Some people are adept at recognizing the worldviews behind at least certain of their activities. I found they could make almost immediate use of this kind of understanding.

However, if one doesn't recognize one's own harmful worldview or can't find the acts sustaining it, it remains unclear how to proceed. My patients found it especially difficult to identify the worldview and reasons for behavior that was habitual.

Then, partly, by accident, I found a way to determine in many cases what habitual behavior means to a person and, in the process, found a stunning form of corroboration that individual habits do indeed each pipe their own special worldview to the mind. There was a way of *deciphering habits on the spot*, ascertaining this worldview—at least the gist of it—and thus utilizing the truths already uncovered.

CHAPTER TEN

The Hunger Illusion

My newfound and dramatic way of interpreting the messages that habits send to the mind came from an unexpected source. There were important truths concealed in the experience people reported having during the first stage of breaking a habit. During this time, as I mentioned, the urge for the activity is powerful. There's a feeling of being starved for it, the activity itself seems more delicious than ever.

There's an illusion to which the person becomes subject that accompanies peaks of the urge. While seeing the activity in its best light, he has a sense of himself as deserving to do the thing or as needing to do it desperately. And the activity itself comes to look reasonable, justified, or even necessary. For instance, a man breaking the habit of repeating himself felt an enormous urge to do so. While restraining himself, he felt absolutely certain that no one could have heard him the first time. This feeling of certainty was a full-scale illusion which accompanied his urge.

The person stopping a habit might have nothing more than a hint of this experience—a sense of embarrassment, for instance, or a feeling of being foolish in the new role. It might be more, a glimpse of the self in society. Although fragmentary, this glimpse would be detailed. For a long time, my mistake had been not to look at those details, or even to elicit them by asking people questions about their experiences at such times. If anything, I had deliberately stayed away from examining this kind of thinking. I was aware that the person often presented these thoughts as an excuse to resume the activity. It hadn't occurred to me that the person *was truly experiencing himself and life in this particular way at the instant,* even if he was also using this view as an excuse for all it was worth.

"What's the difference if I overeat? My husband doesn't love me. There really isn't much else in life." Implicit in this woman's desire to eat would be a whole sense of self according to which she had nothing to lose. It would even be sensible under the circumstances. The excuse bears the logic of the illusion, and the person would often deliver it with a passion borrowed from her urge.

But gradually I saw that I couldn't just sum up such experiences as excuses invented for permission to resume the behavior. This woman would really feel depressed predictably so, each time she went on a diet. We could know in advance that she would feel unworthy of her husband's love, in doubt about him, and about her desirability altogether.

In still other cases, I realized that the idea that these illusions were simply rationalizations was belied by the fact that as excuses they were too flimsy. The person could have done much better if he'd wanted to. An official in Alcoholics Anonymous told me about a man in his second week of quitting drinking, who blurted out to the group, "But I've got to drink with my family on Christmas day. Otherwise, they'll think I don't care about them. That's what we do together." Then one of the other members reminded him that it was only July. He could easily have made a better plea. However, the thought of Christmas and fear of losing touch with his family had come to his mind. Withdrawal from drinking had suddenly produced that fear.

People experienced the same kind of illusion when they forced themselves to do things that they'd wanted to do but had systematically avoided. A woman having sex with a man for the first time could virtually see her mother in the room with them, sobbing and shaking a finger at her. Repetition dimmed the vision. A month later she had moments of panic, and more than once thought she heard a knock on the door, as if sounds from within her were coming from outside. By the end of six months, however, she no longer had to endure this kind of reaction.

What attracted my attention to this kind of illusion was its consistency. The same kind of experience would befall the person time and again when he was fighting the same urge. The same hopeless image came to the woman dieting, for example. Looked at in detail, these reactions proved highly idiosyncratic. I decided to call the phenomenon the *hunger illusion* because it rises along with hunger for the habit and subsides as the person breaks the habit. When the person becomes free of the urge for the activity, this illusion also diminishes and finally disappears.

People might have different kinds of experiences even when stopping what might seem to be the same habit. For instance, I'd talked with several women, who had recognized after attending a feminist lecture that all their lives they had been unduly tentative with men, especially when disagreeing with a man they liked. Commonly, they would preface their opinion apologetically—by saying "Well, it seems to me . . ." Or, "I may be wrong, but . . ." When giving an opinion to another woman, however, they would never bother with this kind of preface and they decided to stop. The lecturer had made them aware that they'd been acting fearfully without knowing it, and the plan was for them simply to state their opinion without apology in any form.

As expected, most felt frightened the first time they stated an opinion directly. But one woman reported feeling unexpectedly sorry for the man. She had walked out of her boss's office picturing him crushed by the torrent of her disagreement, which in reality was quite mild. That night she dreamed of a frail old man in a white shirt, slumped dead at his desk late at night. Her motive for catering to men had been quite different from the others'. She had the particular feeling, that she was annihilating men, in other situations, too.

Although people reacted differently to their stopping what seemed the same activity, the consistency of a person's reactions obviously meant something. These illusions were directly associated with the activity being stopped in each case, and told a good deal about the associated worldview.

I began asking one person after another to temporarily stop habitual behaviors, not always harmful ones, as a way of getting in better touch with their reasons for acting.

Then I saw that implicit in the *hunger illusion* itself was a worldview. Within the illusion the person saw himself as a certain character in a situation that required a particular performance. For instance, he saw himself as not being taken seriously and therefore needing to *repeat* anything of importance; as needing to win a competition by *denying* all mistakes and *pinning* errors on others; as weak and reliant on men and as therefore needing to *satisfy* men by submissive acts. Or as strong and in a world where the men are so weak one must be cautious so as not to upset a man by too much show of strength.

Now that I was eager to investigate the hunger illusion, I was well positioned. It seems almost in the nature of this illusion that, under its spell, people *want* to talk in ways that reveal the illusion. Often, the worldview implicit in the illusion was apparent. When it wasn't, I sometimes felt like a theater critic trying to identify the theme of a play and its real meaning.

Excitingly, the point of view implicit in what the person experienced was *exactly the one soon to undergo change as the person broke the habit!* The denier of mistakes would feel slightly less in jeopardy when he stopped. The women who felt frightened of men at first would feel less so after a while, and the one who'd felt that she was devastating a man by disagreeing with him would think of men as less frail and would not worry so much about her opinions being crushing.

Breaking the habit amounted to a way of tricking its meaning into consciousness. This meant that people could best infer their motives by stopping the activity and studying the ideas that came to mind. They could get an early sense of how quitting the behavior entirely was going to affect their outlook. What befell them at the outset provided an accurate *reverse measure* of how breaking the habit was going to affect them. From the very fact that a man felt unworthy of notice without name-dropping, he could anticipate that when he got rid of the urge entirely, he would feel more sufficient, more worthy of notice. A man who felt guilty over his divorce began to make demands of his children; he could tell from his initial reactions to doing this that if he made such demands regularly he would feel less guilty about his past treatment of the children.

Along the way I began to realize something else: This glimpse into the meaning of a habit, through study of the hunger illusion, was often a return to the person's early past. Not literally, of course. But the picture of life, the one contained in the illusion, often made sense if understood as the person's past way of perceiving his existence.

Recall the man who felt small and unnoticed as he fought his impulse to gesticulate. He'd been the tiny one in the family. Gesturing broadly had served him well. To offset his sense of himself as small and unnoticed had remained at least a partial motive all along; this, in turn, meant that the gesturing had really continued to undermine him. But the amazing thing was that the hunger illusion brought a glimpse of those early days through his eyes. Similarly, the woman afraid of damaging a man recalled such a fear about her father, who had emphysema. He would never enter her world, so she had tried to enter his, catering to him, being sure never to add to his burdens. Past history also spoke to the woman who felt depressed and unloved when she dieted. As a little girl, she would overeat when her parents were not at home. Curbing herself at first brought back that old sense of herself as isolated, unloved.

Naturally, not all a person's associations at such times are historical, but many are. I began pressing people hard to tell me about these illusions. What comes to mind at those moments? What are you afraid of? What do you look like at such times? What will the other person do? What's the worst that can happen? What will be revealed about you? What will happen then? How will that harm you? By doing this repeatedly with some particular pattern of would-be behavior, I could see strong consistency from one time to the next. For instance, for one person the notion of sin would come up often; for another, the fear of hurting people; for another, losing friends; for another, a sense of powerlessness. What I was getting often amounted to a precise picture of how the person felt about himself when acting, though often the person couldn't identify that sense—it wasn't keen enough. The person now felt relief in being able to hold it, to comprehend it, and felt absolutely certain it had somehow been in the atmosphere for a lifetime.

It made no difference whether the worldview, which the habit had been preserving over the years, was originally based on a mistaken notion. Wrong impressions were as readily preserved by ongoing behavior as accurate ones. Stopping the behavior yielded hints of whatever the worldview had been when the intention was formed.

A similar illusion was experienced by people fighting inhibitions. The person was forcing himself to do something he had wanted to do, but had habitually avoided. The past returned even more vividly in these cases. Glimpses into those past times were sometimes as vivid as nightmares. Recall the woman's picture of her mother scolding her for having sex. In her fantasy, her mother was once again gigantic, influential, shaking an accusing finger and with power to carry out her threats. I was seeing her mother through her childhood eyes.

Such visions represented anachronisms. The discrepancy between past and present had enabled me to appreciate that in these cases habits were restoring past impressions. It must be, I realized, that in other instances, where the person has good reason in the present to believe a past message, the past still exerts its influence though it is harder to discern. But I soon realized that even here there is a way to identify this influence.

I was treating a man whose relationship with his mother had changed minimally over the years. She continued to distrust his ability as she had when he was a child. She would insist that he keep her informed of his doings and would thrust advice on him. If he excluded her, she felt hurt and resentful. With her position so much the same, it might seem the man, who doubted his ability and who worried about his relationship with his mother, was forming a contemporary perception of his life. However, I could see that even here, where the person's circumstances had not apparently changed, the past played a role. It gave color to his perception of the present. The *implications* to him of what he perceived still bore the stamp of the past. Suppose he struck off on his own, what was the worst that could happen? To him it seemed, as it had when he was a child, that mistakes are grievous, irreparable, that he could not overcome obstacles, and that he would do more harm to himself than good in the long run. The meaning of his mother's withdrawing from him, his sense of great danger if this happened, also bore the unmistakable stamp of a much earlier worldview. That he saw the present in the light of the past became clear to him only later, when by taking chances he actually changed his worldview.

I realized that when studying people's initial reaction to changing their behavior, I could expect no response to be utterly free of the past. There would be subtle forms of anachronism, even when people were correct in their anticipations of events. These influences from the past could be discerned in what the events seemed to *mean* to them. The person might be right in what he anticipated but wrong in his reasons, or excessive in what he thought the event implied, or in how hopeless the situation seemed, or in how to cope with it.

Years later I studied closely the presence of the hunger illusion in dreams. Time and again when people went against the grain of habitual behavior, and suffered the shock, they had intense dreams. Past figures often came back to haunt them. The jeopardy, the danger they now experienced, was dramatized on the stage of their dream, played by the original cast as they had once appeared. One of Freud's early students, Wilhelm Stekel, once reported that he could get patients to dream by sending them home without a session if they had no dream to report. Perhaps. But I could more than match the technique by asking people to fight some habitual pattern. I think nothing else is so great a prompter of dreams as this experience.

Looked at from this point of view, dreams sometimes suggested motives to me that were utterly unexpected. Of course, any interpretation of dreams is highly conjectural. Yet, as in the following case, I could see the answer once a dream had pointed to it. A woman seemed always to be quarreling with whatever man she had started to feel romantic about. Almost at once, she would find things wrong with him. In addition, she would talk to her friends about him in such unflattering terms, and so insistently, that invariably someone would ask her, "Then why do you go out with him?" and she would reply that the other available men were even worse.

I asked her to do her best for a while not to quarrel with the man she was currently dating and beginning to like. I also asked her not to discuss him with anyone for a time. She agreed. However, she found it harder than she'd anticipated to refrain from talking disparagingly about him. One evening, she felt a strong impulse to pick up the phone just after he'd brought her home. It was easier not to call her friend than to keep off that one burning subject.

That night she dreamt that she was walking hand in hand with her father along a beautiful seashore. The great ocean seemed resting before them and the sun was bright and comforting. He told her that he loved her and she said, "I love you too, daddy." She woke up crying terribly with the urge to go back to him, first to the man in the dream and then when awake to her real father. But he had died some years before. She recalled a childhood in which she had to restrain her feelings for her father because her mother was at odds with him. She had felt great love for him but didn't show it. She kept her joy in him to herself, never showing excitement when he came home and not daring to go places alone with him. Her mother would often disparage the father, and this little girl would pull her emotions out of her expression, say nothing in his behalf—out of loyalty to her mother. It was easiest to argue with him, as her mother did, and in the end she found fault with him too and suppressed her very dangerous love of him.

She had been finding fault with men ever since, making sure that no one would mistake her as liking—or loving— a man. Often her arguing with men, and tearing them down in conversations with her friends, had been motivated by the fear that she would truly care about one of them. This was something the dream had suggested, and which we were easily able to verify in other ways.

Change a behavior pattern and the authorities associated with it, the people you had in mind when you initiated the behavior, are likely to come back in dreams. Sometimes these figures seem like avenging angels. One can easily imagine how primitive people could take such visits as real. They seem so timely. The fact is that we do activate the dead, as they exist in our minds, by changes of behavior.

As a technique for identifying the motives and worldview that underlie a habit, the method of stopping the behavior and studying the illusion is unsurpassed. From the fragmentary feelings and the glimpse of existence that comes to mind at such times, nearly anyone can deepen his self-knowledge. The urge is always clear, and usually the motive. And in many cases the worldview and that glimpse into the past, back to a time when the activity was adopted. Of course, there is room for error, but regular application of the technique to the same pattern of behavior, if it elicits roughly the same outlook much of the time, becomes increasingly reliable as the test is repeated.

Use of the technique often puts people in close touch with some impression they had dimly sensed, held for a long time without identifying it. The person has, for instance, undervalued himself over the years. He or she had taken this appraisal for granted as a reality of life, as something inexpressibly sad, without being truly able to articulate it. Now as the feeling became especially intense, and the conceptualization came to the person clearer than ever, he could see that it was simply a way of looking at life, a perception not necessarily warranted.

CHAPTER ELEVEN

Personality

Personality is thus sustained organically. We are each given to a characteristic way of perceiving ourselves and usual modes of acting, which we recognize only partially. By acting in accordance with judgments already made, we keep informing ourselves that life is a certain way. Our point of view, its whole integration, is alive and receiving nourishment.

A trait, such as stinginess or jealousy or optimism, represents a particular disposition to perceive and act in some way. The stingy behavior is correlated with the way the person feels, with an outlook that is commonly his. The stingy person has unstingy moments, but more than most people he is likely to form perceptions and act in ways that renew stinginess.

Character traits tend to be invisible to whoever holds them. They are adjustments in the lens through which one sees life. The tendency is for our concerns to seem natural, and for the things we stress to seem undeniably to be the most urgent matters in our lives. The stingy man sees himself as reasonable, open-handed, not at all stingy. Other tenants in his building who tip more at Christmas are in better circumstances, he believes. They can afford to do it. The man's perceptions and feelings about himself and life, his dread of danger ahead, and even his impulses to remain stingy—all these comprise the trait.

Let's look at the perception belonging to the trait. The underlying idea might be summed up as, "I have nothing to spare. The main thing in life is never to be caught helpless as my father was." Many of his activities have this idea as part of their message and revive the idea in the mind. Some of this behavior would be described as outright stingy. He refuses to lend his car to a friend in an emergency because he wants to save gas, and rationalizes that the friend has enough money to rent a car. Other of these harmful activities aren't stingy in themselves. But they deepen his self-doubt, and intensify his desire to protect whatever he has. For instance, he holds himself back from pleasurable moments, as by refusing to accept gifts from people. There's a sense that something is to be required of him in return. Few people suspect the reason. To some he even looks generous in his refusals, but those refusals preserve much of the philosophy and way of perceiving that characterizes his stinginess.

A trait is thus composed of a state of mind, which is its involuntary part, and a cluster of habitual voluntary activities. The person with the trait has impulses to engage in these activities, and, if thwarted, to substitute acts from the cluster for one another. There is even a tendency, well annotated by the psychologist Leon Festinger and his colleagues, to avoid confronting data that would throw doubt on one's beliefs, though to a large extent this tendency doubtless varies with the person. Because traits seem solid, it appears as if they motivate behavior but don't depend on it, an important reason to keep the theory in mind. One needs this understanding of pliancy to fully appreciate the organic nature of our ways of perceiving life.

Consistent with our new understanding of causality is the true understanding of what a symptom is. A symptom, if we are to preserve roughly the original connotation, is a consequence, a result and indicator of some cause. Symptoms, like the rash that accompanies a fever, have the property that their removal would not fundamentally change the underlying condition. For us, the true causes are decisions. Symptoms are their consequences. Guilt is a symptom of having gone against one's code. The act is never the symptom, only the feeling is, the perception, the impulse. For instance, a woman crosses the country three times a year to argue with her mother, to persuade her that she is truly more worthy than her brother, whom the mother favors. The woman's need to see her mother and try to win her over is the symptom, whose cause includes behavior such as that of crossing the country to see her.

The more sweeping a trait, the more different behaviors involved, the harder it is for the person to appreciate that it is a trait at all. His overall state of mind makes many adjustments to these diverse activities; the person's philosophy and perception seem in accord with them, as if this philosophy and perception dictated them and there could be no doubt of their wisdom. A habit, a single bad one, might stand out like a black thread in a white tapestry, but the decisions belonging to traits, when there are many such decisions, so influence one's state of mind that after a while it's hard for the person to picture alternatives. "Man does not think he thinks a thing. He simply thinks it is so," wrote Dostoievsky.

The sense of certainty that characterizes traits reflects a property of habits; habits themselves tend to resolve doubt, for better or for worse. Originally, an activity might seem like a reasonable strategy, although not the only possible one; it appears well advised, though there may be other ways of handling the situation. Repetition of a solution tends to convert that sense of possibility toward conviction. Strange as it may seem, acting on a premise makes it seem more likely. Sets of habits do this even more. For instance, a child withholds opinions in the home, having learned that he'll be insulted for giving them. He acquires many techniques to hide his thoughts from people, to remain taciturn, a secret to the world. By engaging in this pattern, now habitually, he confirms his worst fears. As an adult, when he initially forces himself to express an original idea, it seems certain to him that his listeners don't want to hear it.

With traits, the property of certainty becomes even more pronounced. The lens through which the person sees is actually the summary of decisions made, but the lens itself is invisible and there seems no question about the decisions. This absorption into a single, invisible certainty is eminently suited for action.

The evolution of both habits and traits occurring over a lifetime resembles the evolution of human performance over the ages. For instance, some activities and the state of mind that accompanies them are *primitive*, having remained roughly unchanged from the time of their early adoption. A little boy turned his head away sharply from food and also closed his eyes tightly. As a grown man he does the same thing, not in response to a spoonful of food thrust toward him, but as a reaction to unpleasant ideas, for instance. The behavior has hardly been modified from childhood; the man retains the infantile hope that things will just disappear if he refuses to acknowledge them.

Most habits, however, even if continued from childhood, have undergone some *refinement*. The child used to boast openly, sometimes actually seizing adults to get their attention as he told people how wonderful he was. Over the years he has learned to make his proclamations less obvious. He is still excellent at bringing the subject around to himself, but now does it slyly, by introducing the subject of the firm at which he works, for instance, and the loyalty of those under him, a surprising number of underlings. He actually lowers his voice during this refinement of his early brag-gadocio, so that people will feel impressed without realizing that he spoke to them with that intent. The outlook—people will be impressed by me if I bring their attention to my importance—remains from the past. But the style of behavior, the way he restores this attitude, is different from what it was.

Refinements might make history harder for us to trace. But such behavior is historical in the sense that the adult mode is a direct descendant of past practices. What the behavior retains, invariant across all the transitions, is some aspect of the worldview that motivated it and kept it alive. The man's bragging still stems from, and restores, a fundamental unsureness of himself; it keeps alive his dread of being undervalued, of his being unappreciated were he to appear without these boasts, without these stars on his coat which somehow compensate for his inferiority.

The importance of childhood lies in the fact that once a state of mind, a way of perceiving, is established, one tends to search for behavior consistent with it, and to avoid contrary acts. The child, having developed ideas and ways of acting by trial and error, often stimulated by imitation, is in effect solving problems of interpretation and of behavior. If the child expresses this established mode in new ways, with the passage of time the outlook becomes sturdier. It is the way the child is.

For example, the compliant child is convinced that life would be worthless without father's love and that the way to get that love is to act well behaved, never to be disruptive or noisy or to form opinions of his own. As the years go by, the child becomes expert at sensing what people want. He attributes his failures to not having enough of the trait. When others place the child low in their esteem, the real reason is that he has no opinions of his own, he is without adventure. Through his lens, however, as colored by the trait, it seems only that he didn't do enough for people. The impulse is to alter a tactic. The evidence might really argue against an approach taken, but it seldom seems to argue against a person's basic notions or premises about life.

A simple way of stating the matter is that we tend to build on premises we have begun, rather than to start all over again. We vary our approach, compensating for errors as we see them. We reject particular tactics that fail us, but it is unusual to find evidence that calls into question our fundamental premises, those we brought to the experience. In deciding upon particulars of behavior, the child is choosing a worldview he may likely elaborate in years to come, which is why early choices are so important.

Think of the marvelous adaptability for survival the whole process gives human beings. In effect, our earliest character traits evolve by trial and error. The person is predisposed to repeat activities that succeeded and to vary them only when necessary. If the traits themselves, the evolved way of perceiving and feeling, were too flexible, the person would have no identity at all. Character traits thus have the property of being acquired in the real world, of being a record of decisions the person thought fit to make, and they also have the stability necessary to provide a frame of reference so that decisions can be made quickly and smoothly. Such habits of thought, if they are undesirable, can be difficult to change. But the recognition of how they are acquired is the first step to understanding how we can modify our worldview and psyche.

To comprehend personality in this way is to see that there have been no necessarily permanent influences on it. There are no lasting effects, only ones re-created. There is no eternal supply of energy behind any idea, such as hate or affection. Our very appraisal of the value of life, of our own lives, remains subject to change or renewal. One is not denied any form of future psychological life by past events, and if one's way of seeing things appears ineradicable, it is because habitual activities are restoring this way of perceiving.

CHAPTER TWELVE

Repression

A supreme challenge to pliancy is repression, often said to be at the heart of neurosis. In being repressed, have we lost our pliancy? The common point of view, given to us by psychoanalysis, is that this is so. The idea is that by an act of will, the child has banished distasteful ideas or urges, driven them into the unconscious. That act—that repression —now blinds the person to the underlying ideas. Or it nearly does so. Below the surface lie these libidinal urges, retaining some force that would hurtle them into consciousness, but offset, partially or completely, by repressive forces, which also have invested in them an eternal supply of energy. The conflict wages below the surface, and the person feels its results. To the extent that repressive forces succeed, the person loses feelings and freedom, even perception. He does not have the means to see the problem, much less to do anything about it.

Accompanying repression are what psychoanalysts call defense mechanisms, which they explain as consequences of the repression itself. They theorize that the libidinal energy that would have gone into expression of the unwanted impulse must go somewhere. Some of it becomes discharged in the form of new behavior whose function is to protect the person from those very impulses. The force of the impulses becomes used by forces of opposition to them. For instance, a girl wants to strike her mother but instead continually finds fault with her brother. This transferring of object is the defense mechanism of displacement. Were the girl to deliberately act in infantile ways, converting her anger into a kind of demand and also concealing it, this would be the defense mechanism of regression.

Two other characteristics of repression make it tremendously important: its tendency to *last* over many years and its tendency to *spread*. Psychoanalysts construe these as consequences of the repression. Difficulties remain because both repressed and repressive forces have an eternal supply of libidinal energy. That repression lasts implies that the person remains a victim of childhood repressions. That it spreads means to psychoanalysts that it somehow attaches itself to new ideas, which in Freud's words, "come into the same orbit of feeling" as the repressed material. In other words, as the person succeeds in erasing awareness of some fact or experience, he does the same with other facts or experiences, too. Sometimes these other experiences bear an obvious relation to the one repressed. If the person acknowledged them, it would be hard or almost impossible to avoid the repressed truth. On the other hand, repression spreads to facts and experiences whose relationship to the one focally repressed is hard to establish. In many instances, the "orbit" is wide. The girl repressing anger toward her mother does the same with anger toward others. Moreover, she becomes generally listless, as a result of repressing not just anger but healthy aggression too. The repression seems to have left far-reaching traces in her personality.

Freud's scheme thus has the child experience some libidinal urge, usually sexual or aggressive. It seems dangerous to express. By a command of the will, it is banished. But its energy continues to seek discharge. Among the consequences of this are the appearance of defense mechanisms, and also the durability and spread of the repression. According to his scheme, the person has in childhood the power to banish ideas irretrievably, but afterwards remains a victim of having done so. The chief consequences of repression are the symptoms of neurosis.

Let's reconsider those moments in childhood when the decision is made to drive off some experience or idea because it is distasteful. Freud insisted that all primary repressions occur in childhood. One can always interpret any repressed urge as sexual or aggressive, which Freud maintained they were. The real issue, however, is the way repression occurs, not what we decide to call the impulses that are repressed. For instance, a little girl of superb intelligence is constantly embarrassed by knowing answers and doing things better than her brother, who is five years older. Long before she heard the words "mentally retarded," she felt there was something unusual about him in a bad sense. By age five she displayed remarkable memory and ingenuity. On one trip, for example, when the family got lost coming home, she reeled off complicated instructions, recalling the roads they took that afternoon, and reversing the picture to get them home. They responded grimly to her, even unhappily, as if she were drawing attention to the deficiencies of her brother who had been a social failure that afternoon. The parents had seen him playing with boys much younger and being laughed at. Her intelligence, she soon learned, was a real embarrassment to them. Displays of it were something to be controlled, like urination in public. Being smart became painful to her, on this and other occasions, threatening her as it did with isolation.

The stage is set. It is early in life and the girl has strong reason to dissociate herself from an idea, and from feelings that go with it. In this case, the dangerous element is her own intelligence, and whatever is reminiscent of it. It is as unacceptable to her as aggression against a parent might be to another child, or sexuality to another.

So far, the Freudian conditions have been met. How is repression actually accomplished? The classical notion has been that the mind simply banishes distasteful ideas by a command of the will. However, this cannot be done, in childhood or at any other time. To say, "I will not think of this or have this feeling," is insufficient. It is only the starting place. The vow must be followed by action, by many decisions based on it, for the resolution to succeed, even partially. And as one does this—as one carries out repression voluntarily—in exchange for whatever insulation is afforded, there are consequences. There are repercussions within the personality. The child searches for ways of avoiding the particular truth. This means a trial-and-error period spent in finding the actions that protect against it—acts that succeed in dulling the experience or doing away with it entirely: repressive behavior.

Repressive behavior is always motivated by a sense of not being able to cope with an experience, of not being up to it. Along with the fear, there is likely to be a sense of shame. The act is always a decision to protect oneself from the experience, rather than face it. The girl starts to withhold intelligent ideas, says she isn't sure when she really is. She assumes an indifferent approach to studies in school, excels anyhow, but on one occasion deliberately writes wrong answers down on a test. She develops a diffident style, avoids looking at people, and confides in no one. She has successfully repressed her intelligence.

The repressive behavior affords the child relief from the unwanted ideas, but consider its other effects, which we are now in a position to explain. This very behavior, because of the worldview motivating it, restores the person's sense of inadequacy, of not being able to cope with the experience, with the truth, whatever it is. The very flight makes the truth seem more horrible. Flight preserves the worldview associated with flight and the sense of need for it. Moreover, as the behavior becomes habitual, it tends to resolve any doubt the person might have. The girl who thought her intelligence might make her unpopular, after concealing it over the years, feels convinced that this is so. The repetition tends to confirm the underlying notion.

Thus, incredible as it might sound at first, the repressive behavior itself, designed to evade the concern, has the effect of keeping it alive, of keeping the person in a state haunted by it! Chief among repressive activities are the defense mechanisms, which have been regarded merely as consequences—as if the repression could possibly take place prior to such behavior. Ironically, the girl's shunning different subjects in school, her acting childish, were not merely consequences but causes. They kept her feeling afraid of her own intelligence.

It makes no difference whether the child had alternative ways of handling the difficulty back then. The choice to protect oneself confirms the seeming truth of the original idea, sustains the person's belief in it. Despite the persistence of this dread over her lifetime, the power to undo it has never been out of her own hands. What seemed to the psychoanalysts, understandably, like an eternal supply of energy contained in the repressed material was really nothing of the sort. The person himself in every case unknowingly supplies that energy, perennially furnishes the repressed material with its charge. Repressive behavior renews the dread while burying the memory. Every repressed person is repressing *now*.

Of the many unexpected explanations of the events of repression, one is that the same behavior supplies the "energy" for both the repressed and repressive forces. Every act designed to keep an idea out of consciousness also preserves it, and preserves the whole set of impressions attached to that unwanted idea. The person is like someone sending munitions to both sides and keeping a war alive.

Freud's notion that all repression occurs in childhood, and that adult repressions are unconscious repetitions, has been disputed even by psychoanalysts. But the idea that most adult repression is derivative may be true. Doubtless there are new repressions, but on the other hand, people do tend to employ devices that seem to have worked for them in the past. They typically resort to techniques of repression that became habitual for them after they had initiated them in childhood. With our new understanding of repression, the fact that the adult's devices are likely to be repetitions of early learned ones does not spell doom or imply that the essence of repression is over and done with. Repression is a habitual process and as such may be attacked at any stage.

An act of will, the decision to avoid an experience is thus the starting place for repression. But voluntary acts are needed to secure it, acts of the kind that Freud mentioned as defense mechanisms, along with many other activities.

We can sum up the sequence in this way:

1. Unwanted experience
2. Decision to repress it
3. Act of repression
4. Intensification and renewal of dread of it, and of desire to repress it further; renewal of the worldview associated with the repressive act
5. Repetition of this behavior

Repression, of course, is rarely accomplished by repetition of a single act, but rather is maintained by a cluster of behavior with the common aim of avoiding some experience or some recognition of a truth, real or imagined. There is an instant readiness to substitute one method of repression for another if a usual tactic fails for any reason. This insures protection against the unwanted experience, but it also means that the person arrives at multiple ways of adding to the fear of the thing repressed and sustaining the repression.

The spread of repression also relies on voluntary acts. The person, having adopted some repressive device, feels positively tempted to extend its use, and under many conditions is likely to do so. This is especially the case with a child, whose main preparation for new situations consists of recently acquired habits. To the repressed person it may seem that the repression is enveloping more and more of his concerns. There is the sense of being victimized by one's repression, and sometimes by its spread. But the repression cannot attach itself to more of a person's life than the person allows it to. The problem is that, unknowingly, the person acts in the very ways that extend the repression.

Repression spreads in two ways. It is not simply that the repressed material magnetizes other, related, ideas that might prompt the memory of it. True, related ideas become dangerous because the person associates them with the dreaded idea. But what spreads without the person's needing to take action is the dread, not the repression itself. Feeling the dread, the person then uses the same, or other, devices to repress these new stimuli. They too are repressed. He may extend repression to anything reminiscent of an already repressed idea—to an object, another idea, a feeling, to a whole interval of his life that would bring back thoughts of the repressed material.

For instance, a boy is distraught over breaking a vase, an act that he thinks was a reason for his mother's going away forever. He wants to repress the incident. One thing he does is to keep special distance from the remaining blue vase that matches it. He loathes that piece of porcelain, and while growing up makes it his business to stay away from it. Even as an adult, he keeps away from vases, but for reasons he does not understand. It seems to him he just doesn't like them. As an adult, when given a vase of flowers he becomes incredibly uncomfortable without knowing why. Years later he has few memories of the whole nightmarish period when his mother abandoned the family. Without realizing it, he spread the repression, to particulars, to memories of the neighborhood he grew up in, to a whole period of life.

Our disposition to repress anything too brightly reminiscent of an idea already repressed does not tell the whole story, however. The spread occurs in another way, considerably more important. Recall that repression is executed by voluntary behavior. When this behavior becomes habitual, the person tends to use the same devices in new contexts even if they are not reminiscent of the original one. For instance, a man was terrified of looking weak and would repress any sign of incompetence or fault. A usual device of his was to blame others the instant he felt he might have made a mistake himself. Without his knowing it, his doing this over the years kept him feeling his mistakes were intolerable and restored his fear of making them and his expectation of disaster if he were shown lacking. After a while, finding fault with others became easy for him, second nature. He would find fault with friends, in this way repressing impulses to express ideas and feelings quite different from those he originally repressed. For instance, he argued in order to hide warmth. After repressive practices become habitual, the person employs them routinely. The devices themselves extend the repression, they are primary, and it is not necessary that the new ideas being repressed be reminiscent of what has already been repressed.

This spread of repression by new application of old devices is enormously important because it shows the great danger of repression. It can spread without requiring the usual bridge of associations between the originally dreaded idea and new ideas on the horizon. The child who first learns to repress sexuality may use the same devices when there are problems far removed from sexuality. It is not dammed up sexuality but a style of life that makes him a repressed adult.

If we think of the philosophy connected with a worldview, that of repression is the belief that it is better not to know some truths. Acts springing from that belief regenerate the belief, which has many applications in everyday life, if one seeks them. The very idea that it is possible to avoid a truth, that one can do so successfully, by not acknowledging it, is perhaps the single worst outcome of repression. The person applying this philosophy, as the repressed person always does, will do himself harm everywhere in life, intensifying problems, adding to his need for flight, without ever resolving them.

Acts of repression are always in violation of a tenet that Goethe once put this way:

> Even a harmful truth is useful, for it can be harmful only for the moment and will lead to other truths, which must always become more and more useful. Conversely, even a useful untruth is harmful, for it can be useful only for the moment, leading us into other untruths, which become more and more harmful.

It is awesome to think that virtually all the costs of repression are delayed and subtle. It's easy not to notice them. The cards are stacked because the advantage of repressing is felt immediately. Human pliancy presents special difficulties. Curiously, one of the chief consequences of repression is to feel that one's pliancy is lost.

My study of repression illustrates the ability of the whole approach to translate discoveries already made into a new and meaningful form. Seen in this way, the same constellation of events appears as subject to the person's continued control. Indeed, this understanding points to the very methods for utilizing that control.

CHAPTER THIRTEEN

Neurosis

Ordinarily, by neurosis we mean any state marked by some combination of anxiety and compulsive behavior or by obsessions. There is a sense of disunity in the self and impairment in ability to perform. The person is likely to feel divided and disheartened. As Jung put it, "The neurotic has fallen into profound disunity with himself; one side of him wants to suppress, the other to be free." Privation, rigidity, dread of something unknown, hopelessness and a sense of disunity—these might be described as the primary costs of neurosis. Also there is the repeated failure to attain satisfactions that constantly seem within reach and are available to others with much less effort.

The struggle against an expectation of defeat, the need to engage in compulsive rituals to reach what others can seize directly, the distraction and loss of concentration, the demoralization itself, are exhausting. Understandably, people with neurotic complaints often find it hard just to get up in the morning, to be on time, to complete simple tasks in the regions of their repression and elsewhere. Extra activity against an unseen demon, with all its costs, is the very essence of neurosis.

The person would suffer most or all of these losses even if there were no society judging the success or failure of his daily behavior. But there are secondary symptoms: the difficulties of being neurotic in a society where one has to give a good account of oneself.

Anyone in conflict may appear neurotic for a time. However, the presence of conflict is not in itself an indication of neurosis. The inability to resolve conflicts may, on the other hand, not surface at all, as in the case of people who try to handle their neurosis by avoiding conflict of any kind. It has often been maintained that the neurotic actually wants his condition to remain, even if he has the desire to recover from it. No neurotic, it has been said, is undivided in his wish to get well. Evidence for this is the person's continually engaging in behavior that he knows is harmful to him. However, this explanation underestimates people's difficulty in acting in their own best interests, though it is undeniable that some neurotic behavior, such as extreme dependency, can be advantageous to the sufferer as well as disadvantageous.

Neurotic conflict always centers around an unacknowledged part of oneself. The refusal to embrace crucial truths, to face certain of one's own feelings and ideas, lies at the heart of the problem. The various symptoms of neurosis, the forms it takes, are outgrowths of repressive behavior, consequences that the person has not bargained for but nonetheless produces.

Our understanding of repression shows us how neurosis is sustained, and ultimately how it should be attacked. Neurosis is a complex habit-of-mind accomplished by habitual activities and sustained by a network of such activities. The guiding motive, the desire not to see or feel some truth, is sustained in all neurosis. The person continually works to shut out this part of himself, with greater or less success. The symptoms of neurosis are consequences of this effort.

The person with a neurosis encounters three main sources of trouble. First, there are problems that result directly from the return of the repressed material. Secondly, there are problems resulting from the very craving for the repressive behavior, the strenuousness of the efforts needed or, at any rate, expended. Finally, there is the privation and punishment inflicted on oneself by the repression. A person with a neurosis may become subject to different of these troubles, or in some highly defined cases, one form of difficulty is dominant.

First, let's look at problems that result directly from return of the repressed material. Our study of repression has shown that every effort to bury an unacceptable idea, to treat it as if it were intolerable, makes it seem so. Ideas about oneself, a sense of danger attached to them, have been imbued with great force by the behavior. When these ideas manage to return in some form, their meanings are highly charged and frightening.

For instance, a boy grows up with a dread of being wrong. Errors were mimicked and repeated in the home. The boy's father never admitted a mistake. Growing up, the boy covers any weakness or frailty; he responds violently to criticism; he blames other people even before being sure a mistake has been made. Anything to avoid the experience of being at fault. He does this in the office, magnifying his fear of being wrong and all the childhood associations this implies. There will, in his mind, be no recovery from a blunder.

There is a sense of mortification nearly always to be found associated with the repressed material. This accounts for a profound misjudgment of people, especially in the way they view the person and what they expect.

When he is exposed to error, he has pungent moments of anxiety—it almost seems he is having a heart attack. The power his father possessed to mock him, to disqualify him, seems strangely present, as if figures in his present life could, and would, do the same thing. The repressed material is making its return. It might be in the form of anxiety with no thoughts attached. Or it might seem to center around some event that stimulated it. Either way, the historically important part, the characterological part, is what mistakes *mean* to him. Anxiety is the most prominent reminder of repressed material, and perhaps the chiefly observable symptom of neurosis.

Commonly described as anxiety neurosis is the state marked by anxiety itself. The person is either intermittently or persistently unable to avoid experiencing the repressed material. Not knowing why he is so anxious, the sufferer looks for reasons. The tendency is to worry about one small thing after another, as if each were the real cause. Sometimes the thing that prompts this state is the increased desire for the very activity that was repressed, as when a sexually repressed person feels strong sexual urges. In other cases, it is the sudden failure to be able to employ the usual repressive devices.

The second source of trouble is the very craving for the repressive behavior. If it is interrupted for any reason and not replaced at once by other repressive activities, the person becomes subject to acute anxiety. Therefore the person repressing may find himself making great sacrifices to resume the activity.

People show surprising ferocity in attempting to maintain their repressive devices when the devices are threatened. The sexually repressed man, unhappily married, who would like to pretend that the world exists without sexuality, finds this impossible when his daughter's boyfriend visits the home and wants to be alone with her behind closed doors. He'd like to kill that boy. Repressed people commonly displace conflicts, and sometimes appear doggedly constructive. However, where the person seems willing to take nearly any measure to avoid an experience, great cruelty is sometimes the result.

There is compulsive behavior connected with all neurosis —that is, behavior driven by fear and not merely habit. Often the person knows how urgent it is to him to do the thing, even if others don't. The housewife cleans up the apartment before guests arrive. No one thinks much of her doing this, and when they do, they think she is a responsible person. But if anyone stands between her and the cleaning—if someone, for instance, accidentally spills something just before the guests arrive, she undergoes an acute panic. She is symbolically cleaning away a sense that she is worthless, not as good as the guests, and that they will discover this. With the behavior suddenly curtailed or revealed as insufficient, she becomes suddenly exposed to the fear.

Finally, one suffers the privation and punishment that are part of neurosis. Whatever the locus of the dream—sexuality, anger, ambition, dependency—the person has reduced capacity for expressing those impulses and accepting those ideas. Moreover, because people extend repressive behavior, the costs are even greater. The person is often without memories of crucial experiences, the understanding of which might point to a direction for change. If the repression is extremely successful, it may produce a general dulling of perception and feeling. Nearly always, though, the victim has inklings of a problem. The time comes when he wants something in the region of the repression. The sexually repressed person wants a sex life; the person who has long been repressing his aggression finds that he needs it in order to get what he wants.

In these instances the person may never realize fully that he is depriving himself, but he suffers that terrible feeling of disunity that Jung talked about, and often a sense of hopelessness. The repression itself renews this sense, but in addition the person, seeing that his best efforts fail to bring him what he wants, may feel almost like one afflicted with a curse—almost, indeed, as if some verdict rendered back in the past still dooms him.

Suppose, whenever you came close to something you strove

for, someone stationed at your side informed you that you were not entitled to it, that it was wrong, perhaps presumptuous, even to strive for it. The closer you got, the louder the voice became, and it seemed right. When you retreated, went back to being alone though you really wanted intimacy, avoided sex though that was what you wanted, acted compliantly though you had a strong opinion to express, the voice fell silent. It's as if there were safety only in the state of deprivation. Not only would this breed hopelessness, there would also be enormous loss of efficiency even in trying. The skepticism and often the cynicism seen in neurosis are reactions to this sense of hopelessness.

Perhaps the nearest to a pure case of privation is that of phobias. A phobia is a highly specific fear sustained by repressive behavior. For instance, a person whose family was constantly critical of him develops an aversion to any close relationship, and even to the idea of being in a group, which has come to imply that he will be criticized and found wanting. Dread of the phobic stimulus is unlikely to be appreciated unless there is real need to deal with it, causing the person's fear and incapacity to become apparent. When the person is willing to make great sacrifices to avoid having to confront the stimulus, the extent of his fear becomes especially evident. The fear of being in crowded rooms is a common example, though I have never seen a case in which the person limits his evasion pattern to a single object or activity.

Everyone with a neurosis must sometimes weigh these costs. For instance, a man originally trained for the ministry has a terror of stating firm opinions and possibly making other people unhappy. At the mere thought of asserting himself he feels like a dictator, and pictures other people calling him ferocious. He has traditionally handled the problem by withholding opinions, but he now appreciates that this causes him to lose the respect of other people, who see him as a nonentity. When he has a strong opinion and would like to express it, there is danger either way. The person in this position is likely to try one tactic and then the other, finding neither solution adequate. Such quandaries are characteristic of neurosis; it may be easily seen how they add to the person's sense of disunity and how they sap vital energy in everyday life.

The following case shows how a man, by persistently combatting his repressive behavior, enabled himself to identify what he'd been fleeing, and, more important, successfully freed himself of the repression and his neurosis. What was frightening him remained; there emerged an awareness of something he could not turn his back on, an obligation to himself that had gnawed at him, partly because of his efforts to repress it. But the presence of such a problem does not make a person neurotic. Repression is the cause of neurosis with its various symptoms. By battling his repressive behavior, this man rendered himself able to deal with the problem in a nonneurotic way.

At the heart of what he'd repressed was his own ambition. He'd toiled at jobs, though mainly because he wanted no one to have anything to say against him. Among the ways he repressed his ambition were by never asking for a raise or for more responsibility. He would never try to improve himself, as by studying to improve his status. Nor would he talk to people about his hopes for the future or about theirs. Indeed, he did his best to avoid talking about the future altogether, which made him the extreme antiromantic— anything to avoid feeling that he might strive for more. His lashing out at people was a last-ditch defense, which he fell back on when there was serious threat to his repression.

For the last few years he'd been a publicly employed lawyer on salary, working with fifty others. If one of them would show ambition by leaving to start a private practice, he would make snide comments about the person. This helped protect him from a feeling that he himself could be doing more. His wife's friends, too, were a serious threat to his repression. At the start, one has no idea why something is a threat; it is just experienced as such. But actually, as he later realized, these people's accomplishments and interests were what made them dangerous. Some were in the professions; others were going on with their studies. They all admired achievement and sought it openly. His own desire for advancement was activated by their very presence, and he felt shaken. They made repression harder for him.

Even worse than being with them was hearing his wife praise any of them. He felt utterly distraught when she did this. He would sometimes rant at her, saying how much he detested "those artists and bisexuals." Only by stopping his flight, relinquishing these tactics, could he get rid of his neurotic symptoms, the worst of which were chronic anxiety and a sense of despair.

Boldly, he agreed to have these people over to his home. To his surprise, he found himself thinking in a way he'd always associated with his wife, not with himself. It flashed through his mind that his house—the furnishings, the paintings—weren't good enough. They betrayed his low income. It became obvious that it really mattered to him that he hadn't accomplished more. His surrendering a repressive technique had brought him directly to this truth. It was inescapable, and though it hurt at the time, it was invaluable for him to know it. The important thing was to keep describing it accurately to himself—as fear and not as justified contempt for those people.

With the guests present, he felt anxious and retreated to a room alone to think. Tonight, he resolved, he was not going to pick a friendly argument or get drunk. Listening to their joyous voices, he realized what the experience reminded him of—of guests coming to his home when he was a child, mostly to pay homage to his brother, considered the darling. His brother, who had gone through school two years ahead of him, with friends galore, had left a lasting impression. Having the same surname as his brother had brought him a welcome from one teacher after another. They'd expected him to do as well. But what a disappointment he was! How humiliating that phase of childhood had been. Why couldn't his mother love him as he was? Why was it always a matter of working hard to get her approval, like swimming against the tide? He had to smile when he thought about his brother's being a blatant homosexual, the ultimate disappointment to his mother. Two disappointments! And he himself, he thought, had married a woman much like his mother, someone who always wanted more achievement from him.

He sensed having felt this for a long time. But now, as he thought about it, he realized it wasn't so. She would accept him as he was, if only he were happy. He'd been blaming her for nagging him, for being too conventional, when the truth was that he'd been disappointed in himself. To admit that he wanted more would be to confess that he'd been a shirker in life, timid. It had been easier to condemn her than face this possibility. Almost immediately, she looked different to him, more loyal, and strangely, mortal. Stopping a whole repressive pattern also changed his attitude toward her friends, although not immediately. A truth was a truth, whether or not they came to his home to inform him of it. It was clear that he considered *himself* a disappointment. It was a keen awareness now, instead of a gnawing sense. He had localized the problem as his own and could enjoy other people more than he had in many years. The problem remained, but at least he could address it in a nonneurotic way.

Overcoming any repression has pervasive effects on the personality. It isn't just a local change. The person's underlying attitude becomes different. He feels freer elsewhere; he sees himself and others differently. He would perform differently on nearly any psychological test. His style is looser. We are not the same people we were prior to eradicating some repressive tendency. And it is safe to say that everyone has in the course of living overcome at least a few repressions, and felt the difference in his life.

Some people maintain that we have no right to use the word neurotic, that it is presumptuous to call someone healthy or sick. I think it depends on the purpose. True, there has been great danger in diagnoses. They have a way of following people from job to job, or from one mental hospital to another, biasing their chances. On the other hand, we want to understand how people go wrong, how they misuse their pliancy, how they become unwitting victims of their own patterns, so that we can help them discover these patterns and recognize their control over them. We see a person in pain, reaching toward desired objects and pulling back, inflexible. It makes no sense to refuse to distinguish him from the way he might be at another time, or from someone else.

However, when it comes to the activity, unless we understand its role, we cannot call it neurotic. What counts is not the nature of the act but its meaning in the personality, and especially the worldview it sustains. This is important because nearly every modern society at one time or another condemns its deviates, those who do not conform with the majority, as neurotic. An act's being popular in a society does not bear on whether it is neurotic. The person condemned and despised need not suffer from any of the symptoms of neurosis that have been mentioned. And someone else, who produces neurosis in the manner described, will suffer from those symptoms regardless of how his society views him and his behavior.

It should be remembered that what passes as rational in one society may seem neurotic in another. For instance, there are people engaging in compulsions and desperately evading irrational fears, who being in the majority don't ever come to appreciate that they are in this state and that their suffering is avoidable. A usual way people come to learn they have a problem is by observing differences between themselves and others. It's not simply society's judgment that makes the difference, but the fact that once it is rendered and the person loses status, he may attempt to change. Only then may he realize the compulsive nature of the behavior.

Neurotic attitudes toward work and toward death are for

the first time being seen as such. The person who plunges himself into work as an escape from intimacy, or to avoid reflecting on his personal life, may have passed as having no problem relating to work, whatever other difficulties he might suffer. But for such people, working is a repressive act, a form of flight, which becomes apparent when the person stops. The word *workaholic* has begun to appear in popular magazine articles to describe such people.

And the person who lives constantly in dread of death, who never talks about it, who shuns anyone seriously ill, who denies death compulsively as part of his religion, who pretends one way or another that dead people have not really undergone death, he too was more in the majority 20 years ago than now. His evasion of anything reminiscent of death is becoming appreciated as compulsive and neurotic. As with all repressive behavior, this intensifies his dread of the very thing he is fleeing from.

What counts ultimately is not the judgment of society about the aberrant individual, or even the issue of whether he differs from the majority. The real criterion of neurosis is whether he is systematically and compulsively fleeing from an idea or experience, thereby renewing his dread and causing himself to suffer from the other symptoms of neurosis. By doing this, whole societies may repress themselves. They may suffer from impulse disorders with violence just beneath the surface; they may indulge in collective sublimation, be fetishistic or paranoid. Whole societies may suffer from any form of neurosis that can afflict the individual, and for virtually the same reasons. And just as all these conditions are in the individual case sustained unknowingly by the person's voluntary behavior, the same is true in societies. Whole nations have often made themselves neurotic one way or another. But on other occasions societies have overcome enormous psychological problems. They always retain the power to do so, just as individuals do.

The real criteria for neurosis and mental health are intrapsychic; they stand as independent of society as a person's physical health is independent of what is said about him. Society can invite self-destructive behavior, self-hate, neurosis, just as it can command poisonous habits, such as that of eating harmful foods well advertised. By understandable choices, people may damage their mental health as they sometimes do their physical health. But the measure of the health or harm is within the person.

Anxiety, for instance, is commonly produced by the person's acting contrary to some established pattern. There is a heightened consciousness. Along with the established behavior, as part of the old regime, was a philosophy and outlook. Safety seems to reside in doing what one did, even if common sense tells the person that the old way was harmful and the new way better. The very disunity, which stops the neurotic from building dependable habits in the region of difficulty, results in anxiety. Anxiety related to the breaking of patterns is certainly not the only kind we human beings endure. But a great many instances of anxiety are resolvable to this one cause.

Had we begun with the healthy person, the one not repressed or neurotic, then the values of a healthy personality would have been the topic, instead of only being implied by the costs of repression. The resolution of neurosis, mainly by finding and discontinuing repressive activities, nearly always yields enormous benefits. Not everyone would agree on the criteria for mental health, but there is value in setting down measures as a first approximation:

1. *Self-esteem.* Appreciation of and enjoyment of oneself as a human being.
2. *The capacity to experience a wide range of feelings.* The ability to feel not only joy, for example, but also fear and anger.
3. *Spontaneity in expressing feelings and in action.*
4. *Flexibility* to switch from one kind of approach to another as the situation changes. This implies open-

ness to criticism and the capacity to appreciate errors
and profit from them.

5. *Curiosity.* When faced with ignorance, the desire to
increase knowledge rather than retreat in fear.

6. *Independence.* The ability to trust one's own emotions and reactions, even when they seem unconven-
tional or unexpected.

7. *Assertiveness.* The ability to act decisively, without
collapsing and without great guilt or the desire for
atonement.

8. *Courage.* The ability to pursue ideals in spite of fear.

9. *Consistency.* Persistence in patterns of endeavor,
necessary for long-term satisfactions and for a sense
of continuity.

10. *Romanticization of life.* The sense of one's life as
high adventure.

These are complex habits of thought. The creation of
them is always possible by decisions, small ones, which in
accumulation can introduce and strengthen these qualities.

PART THREE
The Practical
Side of Pliancy

The study of human pliancy gives us a new psychology, more hopeful, if sometimes more frightening, in its possibilities. In this section I want to discuss some of its many implications, such as those for self-help, for therapy, for helping a friend, for raising a child. These not only concern what a person can accomplish, they also have important meaning for what the study of psychology itself can achieve.

CHAPTER FOURTEEN

Our Natural Equipment

Of all the faculties thought to distinguish humans from beasts, the richness of human consciousness heads the list. Many people equate consciousness with being alive. To think of it as a faculty may seem odd because consciousness feels inseparable from the self. It is simply there. Over three billion forms of it exist, one for every human being. Yet in all these variations it apparently obeys at least some of the same basic principles.

The nature of consciousness is to flow. It seems ever changing. States of mind succeed one another. As I mentioned, William James likened consciousness to a river or a stream.

We can direct consciousness to an idea or impulse, but we cannot lock it in place. Failing to realize this, many of us think ourselves seriously deficient in the ability to concentrate. Even while addressing ourselves to an important task, our minds will wander.

James took a humane position in describing this aspect of

consciousness and exhorting people to accept it, and to accept themselves in spite of it:

> No matter how brain-scattered the type of a man's successive fields of consciousness may be, if he really cares for a subject, he will return to it incessantly from his incessant wanderings. . . . He will get more results from it than another person whose attention may be more continuous during an interval, but whose passion for that subject is of a more languid and less permanent sort.[35]

Even our most outstanding thinkers find that their minds wander when they work. To acknowledge this property of consciousness—to understand that the mind takes commands but not for long—is to avoid needless self-reproach. In the end, it will be helpful to base strategies on the expectation that the mind will wander. To take fair account that this flow will occur keeps us grounded in reality.

A second property of consciousness is its focus on single ideas. Consciousness can shift its focus rapidly; it can move from one topic to another in rapid alternation. But it has only one significant focus at any time. Sir John Eccles, a foremost authority on the brain, is credited with having called this phenomenon the "unity of consciousness." This unity is truly a miracle of coordination, considering the brain's complexity. Many millions of cells take part in the simplest cortical response, weaving together into a complex pattern that produces such a unity. So far we have only a shadowy picture of the process in which so many nerve cells are activated. This mental unity remains intact even after the appearance of large lesions or surgical destruction of the cerebral hemispheres. Eccles wondered:

> How can this tremendous dispersion of activity . . . in the brain . . . give rise to this unity, and from moment to moment, the relative simplicity of our conscious self, so that the play of experience appears to be, as it were, all on

the stage before one conscious self? (Eccles, Sir John, 19th Arthur Stanley Memorial Lecture, "The brain and the unity of conscious experience." Univ. Press, 1965)

Because of the unity of consciousness, we are actually fortunate that stabilizing consciousness is impossible for us. A voluntary decision would be needed to free consciousness. But the fact of this unity, the single-mindedness of consciousness, implies that there could be no awareness that the time had come for a change. Once locked into an idea, unless consciousness flowed, it would remain forever that way. The flow of consciousness stops us from becoming frozen. For our ancestors the ease with which consciousness flows was a survival trait. The readiness to be distracted by any unusual sight or sound depended on this. For those of us annoyed at our own inability to concentrate better, it may be small consolation, however, to realize that the ancestors of our outstanding concentrators may well have been eaten alive. There are writers who argue that the single-mindedness of consciousness is not pure, that there is a peripheral sense which must be taken into account. Whether or not this is sometimes so, unity is an overwhelmingly important aspect of consciousness.

If people are to change their mental states, their underlying outlooks, by acts of will, they would have to know how. Which acts would make the appropriate contributions?

Medical specialists for their purposes are able to distinguish between *voluntary* and *involuntary* acts. For instance, a person can raise his arm, and in general move skeletal muscles, voluntarily, but cannot govern biochemical functions in the same way. By acts of will, we can direct our thoughts far and wide; we can say what we want to other people, or not speak at all. We cannot, however, suddenly extinguish feelings or exchange them for others. If we dislike someone, we can't by a command from the higher brain center get ourselves to like that person. And if we dislike ourselves or feel incompetent, no single stroke of will, no command from our higher brain center, can get us to feel differently.

The experience of initiating an act seems to coincide closely with what we can actually accomplish voluntarily. The sensation, "I am moving my arm," accompanies the act of moving it. The same correlation between experience and act may be seen from another angle. The explorer of the brain, Wilder Penfield, could by touching a sector cause a patient's arm to move. Such patients would report, "My arm just moved!" and say that they experienced a different feeling from that of moving the arm themselves. Acts of will often entail hesitation beforehand, perhaps a feeling of resolve, as well as a sense of effort. But not always. What seems to distinguish such acts is the sense of a self-in-action as distinguished from a background—the feeling of an "I" making decisions.

Our mental state is revealed to us only in glimpses of consciousness. Whatever that state may be—if, for example, it disposes us to hate ourselves and makes honest effort seem pointless—is likely to affect our consciousness. Or we may not be aware of our own disposition at all. Consciousness may even delude us, misreporting the true condition of things much the way a newspaper might give a false impression of the state of affairs. And we have seen how easy it is to misinterpret consciousness, with the habit illusion. The intention of personality change should always be to improve the basic outlook, never simply to toy with consciousness so that things seem different when they are actually the same. This brings us to some highly practical problems.

CHAPTER FIFTEEN

Self-Help

The pliancy perspective furnishes the point of view ideal for self-help. What we already know, if put into practice, would enable many people to make sweeping personality changes on their own. I believe that this study could do more for people in a short time than psychology has done until now.

Perhaps no two people hold precisely the same attitudes supported by the same activities. And people vary in how ready they are to change particular activities. The best order of attack for one person might not be sensible for another. What is invisible about a problem to one person may be evident to another. But even though tactics must be devised in each case individually, certain things can be said about the overall strategy.

Most contemporary writing on self-help concerns ways of getting ahead by improving social relations. By acting differently, one can acquire friends, earn promotions, even find love. Such concern over the impressions one makes has its place. Other people are important in our lives. But impression-making cannot be the primary project. Our study of pliancy has shown the dangers of trying to improve one's outlook through the indirect route of cultivating other people's favor. There is intrinsic harm in trying to change merely to elicit a different response from other people, to please them or persuade them of something. Where this is the overwhelming reason, the effect is to increase one's dependency on what others think and to need approval more.

In addition, personality problems may not manifest themselves in one's having trouble with others. Neurosis, as we have seen, is essentially an intrapsychic disturbance. The problem would exist even if no one else were disturbed by the neurosis and therefore there were no social signs of difficulty. Certain neurotic patterns find a ready audience, and the person who breaks these patterns may, if anything, find that he is displeasing particular people who expected him to remain as he was.

Something else is needed: a purely private scrutiny of what change in outlook would mean, followed by the decision that it would be worthwhile for one's *own* sake.

The strategy may be thought of as subdivisible into five main phases: the first is to identify the condition to be changed; the second, to pinpoint the controllable acts sustaining the condition; the third, to find an order in which to change activities; the fourth, to refrain from the harmful behavior; and the fifth, to find and engage in the new behavior that will usher in the new way of thinking and sustain it. There can be exceptions, however. It might be that stopping the harmful behavior proves enough, and that no replacement is needed. One can't in practice carry out the stages sequentially. One must double back repeatedly, as when discoveries made at one phase of the work throw light on something that should have been done at an earlier phase.

1. *Describing the problem.*

The problem might be difficulty with stopping a single activity, or it might be the burden of some very general attitude like despair. Either way, one's picture of the problem is almost sure to change as the person makes new discoveries about himself. Usually, the person suffers the recurrent pain of feeling unable to perform satisfactorily, unable to do things up to expectation. He feels a blockage of some kind, along with pessimism. But personality change is too often conceived of as making up for a lack. The desire to enhance qualities already possessed, to increase sources of pleasure, are also valid reasons to contemplate change. Such a venture might be prompted not by pain, but by the recognition that a different outlook would enable one to live more deeply or sensually.

One is especially likely to recognize a harmful attitude while trying to stop an activity. For instance, a man trying to cope with compulsive gambling discovers while forcing himself to stop that he is without a way of impressing people. He feels humiliated, as a man without a winning system, as someone in a humdrum job who may never be rich. For the first time, he can hardly imagine why anyone would like him or even tolerate him. His pervasive feeling of inadequacy is of long standing, but not till he battled a method of repressing it did he discover it.

Many personality difficulties become apparent in relationships. We see how other people react to us and how they differ from us. Using the information, one must then try to define the problem, thinking of the underlying attitude and looking for behavior it might motivate.

2. *Identifying the harmful behavior.*

The critical question is, What do I do in accordance with this unwanted worldview? How do I express it in daily life?

Among the first candidates are any habitual activities that spring from fear. The person feels a compulsion to do the same thing in the same rigid way, even though he sees the obvious disadvantages. But often such behavior is extremely difficult to change if the project is to deal with it first; it becomes more amenable later on. The hard part is to find those small activities supportive of the unwanted attitude which, once discovered, could be dealt with at the cost of only slight anxiety.

While rounding up these crucial activities, it is best to keep trying to describe the unwanted worldview in as much detail as possible. The question may be put this way, Which of my regular activities does this worldview motivate, either completely or partially? Some answers are almost sure to be found at once.

It may help to observe other people who don't have the problem. How might they act in a similar situation? What might they *not* do?

A man, for example, feels weak, undeserving. He watches the way a friend returns a radio that didn't work, and within five minutes discovers about four ways the friend had of putting things that because of his fear would never have occurred to him. He would have begun by saying it was his own fault that he took the radio without trying it. If he could only dispense with apologies and stop anticipating trouble by mentioning it, if he could even allow himself to remain unconvinced of other people's ability and integrity after such an episode—live with this uncertainty about others, he would be healthier. He has found a set of assignments, all of which will be helpful to him.

At this early stage, the person has the problem, is more aware of it than before, but knows only some of the ways he has been restoring it. In the process of changing the behavior, however, a great deal more can be learned about its underlying worldview; this information, in turn, leads to discoveries of new behaviors. What will the man feel like when his time comes to return the radio or to carry out a similar task? He has vowed this time not to apologize or preface his remarks. He will even make a rehearsed statement of what he believes—that the other person was negligent and that he is dissatisfied. Even if he achieves only part of his mission, he is sure to be flooded with thoughts, feelings, and reactions that will tell him a great deal more about his problem and ways he has evolved of expressing it.

It is not necessary to pinpoint all the decisions reproducing an outlook, a habitual way of thinking, to change the outlook. The more activities identified and dealt with deliberately, the better. But it suffices to locate a core of crucial behavior. As the person changes it, and comes to see life differently, there's a tendency to drop old behavior that now seems out of place.

As with any challenge, people bring different qualifications and experience to the problems. For instance, they differ in how well they can pinpoint activities and discover harmful cues. They differ in determination and in openness to emotion. It stands to reason that if a person doesn't register fear, or guide himself by it in daily life, the person will find it hard to design a strategy to make his life less fearful.

Ironically, while restoring an unwanted worldview, the person may find it difficult to discover how he is doing this. I've mentioned several other techniques for finding the crucial actions in books written explicitly on self-help.

3. Finding a ladder of changes to be made.

With nearly all personality problems, one has a sense of difficulty in relinquishing certain activities. At the start, of course, things seem worst, perhaps even hopeless. Often, it is ideal to be able to change small but relevant controllable activities if they can be discovered, and to revise one's own outlook gradually. In this way, one takes the anxiety in tolerable doses. This means finding a satisfactory order in which to make the necessary changes.

The compulsive gambler, for instance, might profit by first attacking his fear of looking poor, of not being able to impress people with great shows of money. After chipping away at this problem for a while, he may find it much easier

to stop gambling. By not seeing the possibilities of simplify-
ing their tasks through unblocking little by little, people
try in harder ways than necessary. With a ladder of changes
set up in order of difficulty stretched in front of them, many
people can progress step by step and make changes that
otherwise seem impossible.

Let's look at an example of such a ladder of changes. A
man has grown up in a family that considers itself sacred,
and thinks of crises in other people's lives as mere dinner
amusement. "Members of our clan come first; other people
are fools; it would be treason not to lie for this clan and
die for it if necessary, and it's assumed we all would": this
philosophy was constantly espoused in his home. His two
older brothers have become alcoholics, and this man, although he has managed to run a successful business, has few
friends. Not surprisingly, he expects trouble from people,
and he shows it. On one job after another, the expectation
of trouble precedes real trouble; one romance after another
also ends abruptly. That he is underpaid in his present job
doesn't bother him; at least he's secure. But his inability to
marry, which he had long explained away by citing the
dearth of decent women, now presents a big problem.

One after another, women have told him that he hates
women, that he doesn't trust them. He has long concealed
his own fear of going on dates and of being alone with a
woman he cares about. They construe his distance as contempt, and at the start he doesn't realize that the underlying
problem is a fear of intimacy. Intimacy looks to him like
treason against the family he feels he needs so much and
also loves. Working essentially on his own, as this man informed me in a letter, he finally realized the broad nature
of his fear.

Imagine that full understanding of his problem were
available to this man at the outset. He would know which
activities to concentrate on, and in what order change could
proceed most smoothly. Here are some of the activities that

would have been at the top of his particular list, behavior useful for him to change and feasible early in the game.

A. On dates with women he counts his money, off alone, or he touches his wallet to be sure it's safe, in response to moments of anxiety.

B. He averts his gaze from people, especially women, when they talk about him or about their feelings for him.

C. He often gives one-word answers to questions, sounding curt, in fear of exposing something about himself and of being harmed.

D. When he pays a visit, he always makes sure to find out where his coat is, so that he can make a quick getaway.

E. Before a big date he would whistle songs he had learned in the army, to give himself the courage he felt he would need. It bolstered him as it had in Vietnam.

Each of these activities was motivated by his fear of intimacy with "strangers"—his fear that he would be disliked and the related worry about betraying those at home and being no longer welcome there. The activities have in common that he would find it easier to stop them than most other activities that did the same harm.

Remember that he could not actually have possessed such a list at the start. Nor could he know for sure how hard it was going to be to make different changes. Discovering what ought to be done and arriving at a good order of attack are part of the task. The approach in the doing is necessarily more indirect than the ideal. What is discovered along the way is used, and the best map, the one that would permit the most direct approach, is most clearly understood at the end, when the work is done. Keeping this in mind, let's look at the next rung of the ladder for this man, harmful behavior he found himself more capable of changing once he had made the "lower" changes, thereby giving him more confidence and more desire for a relationship.

A. He would keep distance from women by interrupting them if they started talking about their feelings for him.

B. He would fall silent whenever a person, man or woman, discussed their feelings about anything and spoke intensely. He felt uncomfortable with anything except neutrality at such times.

C. When he liked a woman, he would help her in a variety of ways, never allowing her to reciprocate. Being indebted in any way seemed to interfere with his chance for a quick getaway if necessary.

D. He would reduce closeness by constantly giving advice. This expressed his belief that people could not really enjoy his company.

By switching from these practices, he afforded himself confidence and a still greater feeling of closeness to people than before. Still further along the line was the readiness to talk candidly to his family about his friends, to tell them that he very much enjoyed some of them. The family had always been jealous of outsiders, felt threatened by them, and he had been echoing their sentiments. But now he felt capable of stating his newfound position to them. No more going along with their derisiveness and pointless suspicion, he decided. Speaking up this way was hard, but not nearly as difficult as it would have been six months before. He had steadily broken down the barrier in his mind between family members, whom he trusted, and people outside, and this step helped him further.

These acts of his, these reversals, were each a blow against paranoia, in the sense of shutting off the nourishment for that point of view. It was hard to find those small but routine decisions that had kept it going, but he was gradually able to spot them and replace them by new decisions that engendered a different point of view. The new decisions paved the way for still others in the same vein.

All decisions based on the unwanted worldview are harmful in that they reintroduce it. Therefore, the important question to ask is, What acts do *I* engage in, which, were it not for this attitude, I would not engage in?

People do not know their motivations exactly, of course, or to the full extent, but such knowledge isn't necessary. With practice, most people can learn to pinpoint them well enough to use the method. Study of the hunger illusion is invaluable. Every activity stopped as a possible nourisher of the unwanted outlook should be scrutinized at least once. Examining one's substitutions or impulses toward them has additional value. The person seriously attacking an outlook should make an actual list of changes and place them in categories of difficulty. New items will be added to the list, sometimes on the lowest rung and sometimes on a rung still difficult to reach.

4. Refraining from the harmful behavior.

This task, of course, is in the doing. One of the hardest parts of the challenge is to spot the impulse in time, but sensitivity develops with continued effort. It helps to find precursors of the activity and use them as cues that the impulse may be coming. For instance, some situation or the sudden experience of a particular sentiment might be dangerous: they've motivated the activity before. If identified repeatedly, they will serve as timely reminders not to repeat the behavior.

A special problem arises when the behavior renewing an outlook now no longer wanted has other motivations of real value to the person. It can be difficult to distinguish what the main motive is in any given instance. There's a tendency to think it's the innocent one when it's really the other. In such cases it's best if the person can refrain from the activity for a time. Stopping altogether can purge the behavior of the unwanted motive. In many cases, once this is done the person can resume the activity without harm.

We have all had trouble breaking even one habit. The prospect of breaking a whole set may seem dismaying. But it turns out that breaking five habits together need not be commensurately harder than breaking one. Or any harder. If the habits involved truly share a worldview, have some underlying motivation in common, breaking the whole set offers many advantages if one is willing to try. There are some great savings of effort in trying to deal with patterns. Much of the work overlaps. Only a slightly greater amount of surveillance is needed to war against a set of related habits than against a single one of the set. There are many more chances within a shorter time to weaken the underlying impulses. The hunger illusion is more intense. The crisis, although severe, is sooner understood and over than if a whole sequence of acts had to be changed in turn. Success with any part of the work helps with the rest. Sometimes it is actually easier to stop a whole set of activities than some single activity belonging to that set.

5. *Activity to create a new outlook.*

Technically, a person can rid himself of neurosis—rid himself of any harmful attitude—by discontinuing the behavior that sustains it. But merely refraining from behavior is not enough to account for a highly developed taste, a lust for life, for any detailed and passionate view of anything. The person must also act in ways that foster this way of thinking.

The two main problems are spotting the moment when some act, when saying "yes" to some impulse would be beneficial, and finding the thing of value to do. The moments for action come when the desired view is there. Even the thankless person has moments of appreciativeness; a stingy person has generous impulses. When watching characters on stage and screen, these people admire appreciativeness and generosity, and are inclined to dislike characters with their own shortcomings. The person who wants to develop the new outlook needs to spot these moments. They may not be vivid at first. They are felt when in the company of certain people more than others, perhaps, or in certain situations that can be identified. It would be valuable to arrange for those conditions, if they don't come often enough, and then to act when they do.

There's a curious form of corroboration that the person can find along the way. Anyone trying systematically to change an outlook important in his thinking encounters a certain kind of bugaboo time and again, the same form of irrational fear. It is as if the same monster beset the person's incursions into the unknown territory over and over. Recall the man who had avoided aggression, subdued himself, and held the picture of himself as a dictator, as a kind of irrational madman, when he made even reasonable requests. In the past, the image came to him after acts that seemed utterly innocent in retrospect, and caused no alarm in anyone but himself. He has built more confidence. He is ready to try some more daring things, to assert his independence, patrol his realm.

Now he can use the bugaboo to advantage. It serves him to know the form of his tendency to distort evidence, to misperceive people. Tomorrow when he forces the showdown with the fellow worker, he will feel tyrannical, unfair; it will seem to him that the worker is shocked. It seems that way now. But this is the very conclusion he should mistrust. In the past, judging his behavior from the solitude of retrospect, he saw that his acts were truly mild, even when he'd considered them atrocities. This time, the very monster that might have driven him back becomes a familiar signpost on the road that he knows he must travel.

A chief obstacle is that acts are needed to acquire a new outlook, timely acts and many of them. Some people find, however, that when moments of the desired impulse, the desired worldview, come to them, they cannot think of how to express the impulse. It's not a matter of their refraining in this instance, but of their lacking a vocabulary of behavior that could install the new point of view. Especially in the beginning, the person needs to learn how to convert the occasional moments of the feeling into an active way of responding. Once the ice is broken, he might easily go on, adding details, activities that nourish his new way of thinking, making it still more his own.

It isn't a straightforward sequence of refraining first and then finding some preferable alternative. Understandably, people are hesitant to give up forms of expression, even harmful ones, until they have other ways of finding the same positive values. Sometimes the divesting must come first, but developing a new outlook can make it much easier to part with self-destructive habits.

Where do such acts—or rather the "ideas" for such acts— come from? An example shows the significance of this question.

A woman feels remote from her grandchildren and from the younger generation generally. She wants to cultivate more lightheartedness, and has taken seriously the criticism that she worries too much about people's health and about their doing the right thing. She had used that worry as a device to make herself seem indispensable, and also as a way of expressing love. She had a sudden rush of great warmth toward one of her grandchildren when he visits her in the kitchen while she's at work. But she has no way of expressing it. Another person might in that instant express the warmth, run her hand through the boy's hair, for example. Such an act, however, is not in this woman's vocabulary. She has not thought of it, certainly not as an act befitting her. It is simply not in her vocabulary of ideas for action.

The rare moment of her having this feeling is lost, whereas someone else might prolong it, not just at the time but for later, by acting in some affectionate way. When asked, she reports that it would be hard for her to do. The sense of herself as wrinkled and ridiculous comes to her, the bugaboo, the very sign that she may be on the right road.

Where are people to find the vocabulary of such acts? Watching other people, observing how they express particular kinds of emotions, is an important source. Sometimes the mere willingness to say out loud how one feels, when there is some strong, previously dreaded sentiment, can help the person accept this sentiment. Sometimes invention is needed. The person when alone can think of things to do that might express a particular feeling, and then wait and act in these ways when the feeling comes.

To climb the ladder so as to afford oneself the new perspective, definite acts are needed. Thoughts, as we've seen, aren't enough. Enactment of those thoughts is essential for change. For instance, a man decides 50 times not to compromise himself in a business deal. Then he consents to some compromise. His enactment of the decision affects his outlook, whereas 50 resolutions did not. This means a person can't merely think his way up a ladder of personality change. Merely thinking doesn't permit discovery of the ladder in the first place, but even if the ladder were there, the person would need to climb it. And "climb" means to engage in acts other than thinking. It means to "do" things, in the usual sense of the word: to move out limbs meaningfully, and especially to talk.

Natural selection preserved the distinction between thought and overt action, possibly because of the immunity that it offered to thought. Our ancestors could let their imaginations fly anywhere, cast about for ideas whimsically, irresponsibly, yearningly, creatively, without real danger to their outlook. They could then return to much the same outlook as before the flight of imagination. Thought is free in this most important sense. That actions are needed for change assured that basic changes in the person's outlook would occur slowly. Some discovery, real or imagined, could make one's previous point of view seem very wrong, undesirable. But the person couldn't, in an unappreciative moment or a forgetful one, annihilate his previous point of view. It would adhere—the product of many decisions enacted over a period of time. The old regime, the old way of looking at things, would remain, even if at the time the new idea seemed more accurate. It would take repeated affirmation of this new discovery, whatever it was, for the person to assimilate it into the mainstream of his point of view.

Left unresolved are numerous specific questions whose answers could improve technique in different ways. But applying even what we already know could enable people, *many* people to bring about real and beneficial changes in themselves. And if psychology took up the study and made its findings generally known, many more people could profit.

Psychology could teach people both to think about their outlook and to picture it forming out of voluntary behavior. This alone would make it easier for people at nearly every stage of self-improvement. It could point out obstacles and impart techniques for defining problems and finding harmful actions, for constructing a ladder of change and ascending it. Essentially, if work were done along these lines, the field could provide help of two kinds: it could provide people with precedents and it could offer new theoretical discoveries about pliancy that would amplify, and perhaps correct, what now seems like our basic understanding.

Think first about the usefulness of precedents. Take the man suffering from mild paranoia, whom I mentioned earlier. Suppose he were taught from early life that personality qualities, such as suspiciousness, were sustained by actions. Now as he thought about his viewpoint, the concept would not be new. There would be records of precedents—that is, case histories of people who produced paranoia in similar ways and suffered similarly. Which activities poisoned their minds? Which ones did they feel most able to deal with first? What were their reactions when they felt vulnerable and the signs that told them they were going through a paranoid experience? How did they build their ladder and ascend it?

The person could sift through this information to spot activities that might be harming him. Not that he would automatically find all his crucial behaviors among those listed, even if there were a volume of behaviors to look through. But some of his ways would almost surely be there, perhaps many, and other idiosyncratic ways he made himself paranoid might be easier to discover.

Doubtless there will always be people who either can't or won't recognize their problems, or who can't deal with them. And there will be people who find insurmountable obstacles at different stages, some who can't find the cluster of crucial decisions, or perhaps others who can find some but can't locate enough small ones to start gradually and build the strength to combat some powerful compulsion that pesters them. On the other hand, new discoveries we make about our capability of changing can improve our techniques. What we learn can be given to people to help them accomplish change. Every discovery relating precursors of an act to its effect on the mind can help people at different stages. People could use the information to tell in advance how certain contemplated acts might affect them, and to guide them in launching their attack. There are an enormous number of questions whose answers would illuminate the way.

If not psychology, which discipline can best study the effects of choices on the mind?

CHAPTER SIXTEEN

What We Learn From Literature

"Art is an attempt through description, at pure knowledge."

Albert Camus, Notebooks

Virtually all fiction studies consciousness and assumes human freedom. It investigates the relationships between ideas, feelings, aspirations—in short, it delves into the psyche more deeply than most "official" psychological writing does, and more than the whole branch of psychology that requires experimental verifiability as a criterion. Verification in literature is an individual matter, necessarily. It lies in the reader's recognizing a pattern well enough to identify with some lead figure, or at least enough to experience his struggle.

Great writers—novelists, poets, dramatists—hold the human being as special because of his consciousness. Indeed, the profoundest studies of consciousness are largely to be found in literary works. The Irish poet and dramatist Lord Dunsany once observed that psychologists are like road menders, going a few inches below the surface, while literary masters, like miners, go a mile below. Literature characteristically credits people with freedom. It studies the individual and not the group. The insights of literature are often insights into how people affect themselves. Good fiction is seldom didactic, of course, but writers are continually aware of how characters affect their psyches by their own decisions, and they rely on their knowledge of the ways in which characters undergo change in creating drama.

There is excellent predictability of the impact of great art, because it is grounded in important reality. If an ancient Greek could know exactly how a modern Broadway audience will feel, which character they will cherish; if the ancient could feel our tenderest moments and contrive to make them occur, perhaps even awaken new sensibilities in us, the cable across the ages must be composed of something very sturdy. It is made up of psychological truths.

Psychology has, especially in the last 20 years, withdrawn a great distance from literature. The more scientific it has become, the less it has been able to use the insights of literature. A whole body of knowledge, potentially of enormous importance, became lost to it. The vigor and possibility in human life that literature suggests, the innumerable insights it might afford, seem something apart from psychology. The essential fatalism of modern psychology has rendered it unable to enlarge its knowledge of the psyche from the insights of our storytellers. Psychoanalysts have done in-depth studies of fiction and even of some literary figures, looking at them as if they were real. There has been no dearth of analyses of people's lives, in the vein of Freud's psychoanalytic study of Leonardo da Vinci. With psychoanalysis, however, the aim has been to show the application of principles already believed. The psychoanalyst uses his hypotheses to explain his subject matter, the way a medical doctor might use theories he already holds to understand a patient's ills. This approach is quite different from studying literary works, or biographies, in order to learn from them, and then applying this learning elsewhere.

Take, for example, the twentieth-century French writers Proust, Colette, Maurois, and Gide, whose penetrating studies of jealousy make a collective masterpiece. These writers sometimes have their characters develop jealousy to enormous proportions by acting in different ways that magnify it. The novelist often investigates how people behave and why, and how they harm themselves. Often, the writer's challenge is to comprehend the nature of some problem, to conjure up the details, to make it familiar, if exaggerated. The success of the story or novel depends on its vigor and reality. In reading the work of these people, a person struggling with jealousy might learn a great deal.

Psychology, however, sees the cause-and-effect cycle differently from both author and reader. Preoccupied largely with looking for the roots of a problem like jealousy, psychology views a person's jealous behavior essentially as a manifestation, say of harmful childhood experiences or of some deep-rooted problem. There is serious loss when the insights of the most astute thinkers and best observers of human beings are useless to the system that is supposed to explain human behavior. To say we learn more about jealousy from novels than from psychology is an understatement: we learn virtually everything we know about jealousy from our own experience and from reading fiction; we learn virtually nothing from psychology.

This is because we, as well as the novelist, think of human beings as acting with freedom and as affecting themselves. This viewpoint is fundamental in writing. The audience makes the assumption automatically, and the skilled writer makes it as soon as he starts thinking about his plot.

Aristotle was the first to make us aware of a powerful synthesis between choice and the inevitability of consequences, which becomes the heartbeat of many great plays. These assumptions about the protagonist and those a person must make about himself in everyday life are closely analogous. The protagonist makes a choice—or in ancient tragedy, has in the past made an important choice—and that choice carries inevitable consequences. The audience feels the force of this inevitability, which actually makes the hero's choices more important. Even the incompetent character, whose nature is to lose the struggle, Don Quixote or a Woody Allen prototype, strives for some ideal, is assumed to be capable of choice, and we watch the consequences. What the heroic lead figure has in common with the idealist or incompetent is that by his own struggles he creates complications that then require further mustering of his personal capacities.

Here are a set of criteria for successful fiction suggested by Scott Meredith, expert on the novel and one of the top literary agents in the United States.

1. There's a sympathetic lead character whose viewpoint the reader will adopt.
2. He's confronted by a problem disrupting his life and must do something.
3. Out of the hero's efforts to cope with the problem come a series of complications, which make things seem even more difficult than at the start.
4. The complications rise to a point of crisis. There's a now-or-never challenge.
5. The protagonist acts, either overcoming the problem or failing, but if so, discovering some new truth.

In the end, the protagonist is freed of the necessity to act: he has completed the effort. This comes very close to the experience we recognize when trying to alter any style of life, when the obstacles to be dealt with exist entirely within our own psyches. The person—whether breaking a single habit or setting out to change a pervasive trait—becomes his own lead character. Even in the case of a habit, the very effort creates complications that result in a crisis. Continued effort ends the crisis; the habit is broken, the pattern is changed. If the person quits, resigning himself to the old pattern, this too ends the episode; the crisis dissipates. Either way, the effort has led to complications and crisis, which the person terminates.

The reader, of course, need not know any of this. But the plot that holds to this course has great opportunity. In identifying with heroes of fiction, we invest them with consciousness and will, and the effects that their decisions exert are important to the plot. Usually, the main story concerns external events to which the characters react; one would retell the play not in terms of how a character came to feel, but by giving a chronicle of things that were done, observable things. However, it is a testimony to our interest in fictional characters' inner lives, and the changes they undergo, that even the most dramatic plots of external action, told to nonreflective people (for instance, Shakespeare's "groundlings," eager for action) include considerable examination of the characters' inner lives. In the case of a static character, like James Bond, his very impassiveness and freedom from the usual emotions may fascinate us. Bond's equanimity in the face of mortal danger or while seducing a gorgeous woman, his casual adaptations to the unexpected, make him preternatural. We marvel each time at how events in the character's life fail to affect him.

For some fiction the exploration of consciousness suffices. The American author Henry James was the foremost influence in this direction, showing in his novels and stories how powerful a study of consciousness can be even without sensational external events. Small decisions affect his characters sweepingly, sometimes the decision *not* to do a thing has repercussions throughout the rest of the person's life. With the study of private experience taking on more importance, the everyday character becomes eligible as a protagonist. I think our interest in such people stems not just from our desire for authentication ourselves, but from the desire to learn from their experiences, from their choices, and from how these choices affected their lives.

As viewers of a work, we are supposed to take it as alive; the play is still incomplete when the curtain falls after the first act, its outcome still subject to what the characters decide to do. Such is our reaction when caught up in a work. Psychology, to the extent that it is deterministic, actually detracts from our ability to experience it this way. Its attributing historical causes to the characters and searching for them amounts to saying that the characters on stage were fully motivated before the play began, and are now merely playing out their personalities. It reduces the active to the static. By contrast, the psychology that makes the writer's assumptions about people can reap continuous benefit from the observations of literature. Our purposes differ—that of art is to create experience, nothing more. Ours is to arrive at general laws through specifics, affording us a system that is both explanatory and useful.

And yet art can help us arrive at this system; it can help us comprehend and master our own pliancy. What the poet Allen Ginsberg called the "electricity" of a line is something we feel. Its power to encapsulate and inspire makes it a conceptual shorthand for complex emotional experience.

The psychology bent on identifying the subtler and more powerful forces at play within us can hardly afford to neglect poetry. The poet Karl Shapiro has called poetry "a version of nature and of human nature." The poet's penetration and acuity in observing his own makeup can shorten the psychologist's process of inquiry. Many poetic lines, whether they appear in novels, plays, stories, films, or in poetry itself, make the boldest incursions into the human spirit, bringing back truth, some moment of revelation captured for all to see. The poet who sees it once, in a flash, and can write it down, preserves it better than science can.

Think about the line of Shelley: "Fame is love disguised." With it in mind, I listened to a young man, feeling utterly alone, tell me about the great deeds he would do some day. He would become a foremost inventor, and have a woman fall in love with him. "Not till then?" I asked. The sad truth emerged in the following minutes, that as he saw it, no one could love him unless he were famous. Others might be lovable with less, but not him. With that attitude he could not seek love: he felt he was not entitled to it. Besides, resting so heavily on fame made him inflexible, less inventive than he later became. The ultimate outcome of his work mattered too much, and the doing not enough. I quoted the line to him, and he felt it deeply. A next step was to see where he was not pursuing intimacy that he wanted, where he was waiting and burdening himself with the need to accomplish high deeds before intimacy began. If the poet said it better, more memorably, more forcefully, then our having the poet's words is a great help. Although the purposes of literature and psychology differ, their points of view ought to be more closely aligned than they are.

Many observations that have had virtually no immediate usefulness to psychology are for us important insights into how people can change. Indeed, whenever a writer makes us aware of some unappreciated correlation between idea and act, we have a real use for the observation. Take Samuel Johnson's remark about certain people as "disguising their insignificance with the dignity of hurry." Although this is a penetrating observation of certain people, ordinary psychology has little use for it. The mere discovery of a motive, a chief purpose of modern psychology, has proved essentially a dead end. The great corpus of such discoveries offered by literature has therefore not been worth a great deal to psychology. It illuminates, but that is all. Psychology has itself been grappling unsuccessfully with the matter of changing people's motives once they are understood and seen as harmful.

From our point of view, however, where the statement holds, it lights the way to change for those who care to make use of it. Since hurrying is voluntary, the statement makes clear that for these people, "hurry" must restore or intensify a feeling of being personally insignificant. Every revealing of a motive for behavior is simultaneously a prediction about how that behavior is going to affect the person's outlook. Thus, every such discovery brings the person closer to mastery over his own pliancy. When we examine insights in this way—that is, keep in mind that the voluntary behavior is a *recurrent cause* of the mental state, and not just an expression of it—the same body of insights offered by literature becomes enormously useful to people. Just as the French writers have in effect taught us how people make themselves insanely jealous, Johnson gives information that can help us understand how certain people make themselves feel insignificant. Not that he necessarily thought of his statement as doing this, but we are able to use it this way. Similarly, a whole body of observations becomes useful to us.

The same perceptual scheme is also the best for learning from other people's lives. The deterministic view psychology usually takes, especially psychoanalysis, has not been a help. Why did da Vinci so often leave works unfinished? If we try to answer the question as psychoanalysis did, by looking for qualities already present in the young da Vinci that gave him the personality of a "non-finisher," we are saying in effect that he was destined by his character not to be able to finish his work. Some of us, it would follow, are so destined and others are not.

But within our scheme, we regard early influences as relevant to the track he chose but not determinative. Da Vinci's choices along the way, real choices, made it harder or easier for him to finish his paintings, made it seem urgent to him that he finish them or a matter of indifference at the time. Which choices were they? Holding this view, perhaps we can find some of those choices and learn from them. For instance, did the fact that he readily showed his unfinished work to admirers make it harder for him to finish it? Perhaps. We know that Michelangelo, his contemporary, was so vehemently opposed to letting anyone see his work in progress that he once dove to put out the only light in the room to conceal an incomplete statue from a fellow artist who arrived unexpectedly. It's impossible to be sure which of his choices affected da Vinci's mind in particular ways. But the point is that he did affect himself continually. While he lived, he had real freedom and influenced himself by his choices, just as the rest of us do. If we are to learn from his life, it must be from the choices he made and from seeing how they affected him.

In this chapter, I've talked mostly about writers and the contribution they can make to our understanding of psychology. Till the end of time we will be learning about psychology from nonprofessionals. Anyone who has kept a log of the journey of his soul, or who observes behavior keenly, can give us valuable information. The nature of the psyche is such that any lone individual, looking deeply into his own reactions, might discover a universal truth.

CHAPTER SEVENTEEN

Psychotherapy

*"If you **had** the will and only lacked the strength,*
I could have helped you."

                       Henrik Ibsen, Brand

    The study of pliancy, of how people affect themselves, has exciting implications for the practice of psychotherapy. It shows precisely how a therapist can be most helpful to patients. The essential role of the therapist should be to help the patient see his own potentialities and use them. The understanding of how people produce psychological change provides the foundation for this method, according to which the patient becomes increasingly aware of his influence over himself from the first day. Although he works with a therapist, the patient learns to recognize his command over his life; he produces the cure. Moreover, the patient sees along the way how he is producing it and can therefore preserve his gains and utilize such methods elsewhere in his life if necessary.

Even if it were common knowledge that people create their outlook and sustain it by decisions, and even if the general principles explaining how to do this were widely known, there would doubtless still be real need for psychotherapy. Not everyone could grasp the method. Nor could all those who did, identify their own problems and carry out the steps. Some people would find themselves unable to recognize the biases or tendencies that harmed them. Others would lose sight of their purpose or might falter at any of the necessary steps.

Psychotherapists are presently in a dilemma. If you listen to them talk, you see they are not nearly so deterministic as they once were. Privately, many believe that a patient's decisions regarding his own life can carry great importance. In sessions, they may on occasion exhort a patient to act, to attack a challenge so as to build courage, or to go among people to reduce loneliness or to be assertive so as not to feel cheated. Every sensitive person who works with others sees sometimes that what people do affects them. The therapist knows too that his own choices sometimes affect his psyche and has been aware of causing such effects in himself.

But so far every explanatory system underlying a form of therapeutic practice is deterministic. One sees the determinism in the very *purpose* of these explanatory systems— to account for the patient's behavior. Whether attributed to an Oedipus complex or competitive fear, to the person's infantile needs or social forces, the patient's behavior is seen as dictated by his condition. Psychological systems differ in the ways they account for behavior. That, in fact, is their primary difference. What they share is the purpose of accounting for it. It is implicit that full understanding would make the person's behavior predictable and that the better the system, the more behavior it can explain.

The therapist's dilemma is between the determinism of whatever system of psychology underlies his method and his private beliefs about people. It is a reflection of the choice that any psychological theoretician might have between thinking of himself as free, as is necessary in daily life, and thinking of himself as behaving according to the laws given by his system. It's as if psychology, being deterministic, were a form of training not to speak our native language.

Actually, psychology ought to aim at learning about pliancy and helping people grasp the concept. The therapist thoroughly versed in the pliancy point of view does this just by his formulations and questions. The same material remains important: the person's feelings, ideas, motivations, even his past sometimes. But a new way of looking at them becomes crucial for progress. This new understanding is a steady beam lighting the patient's way—eternally and honestly hopeful.

The therapist with this understanding can help the patient appreciate the mastery he has over his life. During treatment, the patient comes to see the value of this new way of viewing himself and the liberation it provides. Within this therapy, nothing is held back. The therapist has no hidden strategy, makes no interpretations that the patient cannot verify. All truths must come under the patient's scrutiny, since only the patient can use them for cure.

One can imagine a patient who has defined his problem before arriving, and whose work with the therapist is nothing more than a simple extension of self-help. The therapist helps out at the different stages—aiding the patient to spot cues to harmful behavior, for instance, or recording the patient's free associations when he is trying out new behavior.

But in actuality, therapy always turns out to be more complicated. New obstacles are discovered. One finds better formulations of problems. It emerges, for instance, that some special difficulty that drove the patient into therapy is an instance of a larger one. Nearly always the therapist must address himself to the patient's very mode of attacking problems. The patient might, for example, characteristically repress them, making them seem worse. Coping with the repression itself would in this case be necessary for the patient to develop confidence and clarity of perception.

In practice, psychotherapy is always more than just a higher form of self-help, one carried out with the aid of a second person. The very presence of a therapist indicates a relationship and the possibility of biases on both sides. One form of bias has to do with the patient's imposing preconceptions on the therapist and misperceiving him—the transference. Another is the therapist's doing the same with the patient—the counter-transference. There is also the complication introduced by the patient's attempts to subvert progress while the therapist works for it—what has been traditionally called resistance. These, as psychoanalysis has maintained, are perhaps the three vital parameters of the process for the therapist to watch—the patient's transference and resistances, and his own possible counter-transference reactions.

The study of pliancy explains all three in a way that reveals how the participants have control over them.

Let's look at transference first. Recall the psychoanalytic conceptualization of transference as those aspects of the patient's perceptions and feelings about the analyst that result not from their interaction but from the patient's past. For instance, a man assumes that his therapist, a woman, would be shocked if he talked about sex, especially about masturbation. He imagines that, feeling hurt by such talk, she would withdraw from him and remain disappointed with him for a long time. He thus projects onto the therapist the responses his mother had when he was a little boy. People transfer expectations of past figures, especially parents, to the therapist.

By examining the transference, the therapist can learn a great deal about the patient's motives and expectations, even about his past. For instance, the man's expectation of shocking the woman therapist could be safely interpreted as informative about his past. The analyst learns from the transference about the patient's perception of himself as a child, and about his relationship with his mother, or at least about how he experienced that relationship. By analyzing his present reactions, the patient can re-experience those early emotions, can feel them firsthand in a context where they have no justification.

Transference, having been first a property of psychoanalysis, has always been interpreted deterministically. It has been thought that the patient's character structure simply keeps on producing it, forcing the person to misperceive as he does. By this reasoning, the patient's behavior with the therapist and his feelings about the therapist are merely consequences. Many psychoanalysts suggest that the resolution of transference is necessary for cure, and some think it is the only means of cure. The classic question has been how to resolve transference.

In actuality, the patient enters therapy not just with certain expectations and ways of perceiving people, but also with a set of propensities to act in particular ways. His appraisal of the therapist may be dimly etched at the start. But on the basis of judgments made in relation to the therapist, he produces increasingly strong impressions of him. The patient's behavior during therapy, in and outside of the sessions, is the immediate controllable cause of the transference, determining its intensity and its form.

This is why transference grows during treatment. For example, by choosing not to discuss his sex life with the therapist, the patient strengthened his conviction that such talk would have offended her. He *caused himself* to perceive her increasingly as like his mother. The real source of projection is the patient's voluntary behavior; by acting in accordance with perceptions of the therapist, or even with conjectures about the therapist, the patient reinforces them. If, however, the man discusses his sex life with the therapist, the talk will reduce his perception of her as like his mother. It is not just that she will prove more receptive than his mother would have been. Even if she were to say nothing, he would have begun to teach himself that she is a different kind of person. Thus transference, though vivid and firsthand and emotional, merely represents another form of outlook the patient creates, brings from his past, and projects into his own mind by behavior.

Since the patient is always the contemporary producer of the transference, only the patient himself can resolve it.

Some transference is readily detectable as harmful. Where it entails withholding information from the therapist or the use of any tactics that defeat the inquiry, it is evidently so. But what about a patient who unhesitatingly credits the therapist with the omniscience his parent once seemed to possess? Blind loyalty to the therapist, and even to the treatment method, occurring as part of the transference, might seem to be useful, at least for a while. The patient tries hard for someone so important to him.

It has been customary for therapists to utilize this idealization, even idolatry, rather than hack at the roots of so strong a motive for changing. Many therapists have recommended postponing work on the transference, allowing the patient this kind of distortion as if he needed it. It seems to me, however, that in doing this, one is like the medieval priests, who justified "pious frauds" on the grounds that they were good for people's religiosity and for their ultimate welfare. The therapist, in acting on the premise of disbelief in the patient's ability to deal with reality, will perpetuate such disbelief and it will manifest itself elsewhere. There is no problem so big it can't be broached, and the patient can decide whether he wants to consider it.

The trouble is that virtually all views of other people carry implications about oneself. The patient who needs to consider his therapist a god is to that extent himself diminished. That he cannot save himself, and is not actually producing the changes along the way, is implicit. Much transference, although not all, involves the patient's loss of appreciation of his own freedom and capacities.

Most seasoned therapists see the danger in accepting too much credit for gain: The patient gives himself too little. After thanking the therapist on a good day, the patient suffers a bad period, suffers what looks like a relapse. With his philosophy, it seems the therapist is at fault. Not that being blamed is so bad; it's something every therapist gets used to. But the patient is without a proper sense of the ways in which he himself has contributed to either the relapse or improvement.

In a case I supervised, a young addict was being counseled by a man who at 26 was the same age the patient's brother would have been had he not died of a drug overdose. The counselor reported, "He keeps saying I'm his only hope. I'm perfect. I'm that brother." The younger boy was doing well, once again getting jobs as a carpenter, after five years lost. This counselor was truly an inspiration. Was it time to resolve the transference?

An example like this might seem to justify manipulation, to tax the theory about truth. At a staff conference, I asserted that it was time to bring it to the patient's attention. "He counted on his brother, and look what happened to both of them. He's got to learn to count on himself." I argued that the young man loved the counselor. But could he not go on loving him, this time for qualities such as loyalty and steadiness and for his deep concern about the boy? The counselor had already been an important model for him. Why not copy that model in another way—by developing a sense of independence and sufficiency such as the counselor had?

"You think I'm God!" the counselor said, off the cuff, about a week later to the boy. "You underestimate yourself." At other times, when the boy would thank him for help, as he did when qualifying for the carpenter's union, the counselor would remind him, "Did I accomplish that or did you?"

It took considerable time for the patient to resolve this transference, but there were various other benefits in his doing so. In the process it was discovered that the transference also included a vestigial belief that the counselor might be truly frail, start taking drugs, and die the way his brother had. Such acts as asking after the counselor's health were among a set that kept this perception alive. The patient even had a dream of saving the counselor's life from local toughs, and then discovered a sense of the need to prove himself to the counselor in ways that burdened him unnecessarily. Resolving this transference was necessary for the patient's full recognition of his own capacities; by so doing, he became free of concerns he might otherwise have brought to new close relationships, concerns that had been warranted about his brother but that were no longer justified in his life. Resolving the transference distortions may not be the first order of the day. That is up to the patient to decide. But true clarity depends on the resolution, and if the patient wants to work for such clarity early, so much the better.

In the same sense, what is called "counter-transference," the therapist's own disposition to see the patient in particular ways, results from the therapist's behavior. With counter-transference, the therapist projects onto the patient some special expectations not attributable to the patient's actual behavior. In the case of so-called negative counter-transference, the therapist may seem disappointed and angry, or unresponsive to gain. If he unduly favors the patient, this can mean exempting the patient too easily and overlooking actual choices the patient is making to his detriment. For instance, some male therapists are disposed to misperceive their women patients as helpless and easily hurt. Especially with a woman patient who appealed to their mercy, such a therapist might refrain from asking important questions rather than touch a sore point. Discontinuing this form of gallantry after discovering it, would prove a necessary step in their resolving the counter-transference distortion that limits their effectiveness.

In the case of *resistances,* the patient wants to avoid facing some painful truth, or imagined truth, about himself. The therapist is seen as threatening to reveal that truth, by discovering it, bringing it up, or even by innocently leading the patient toward seeing it himself. Resistances are thus forms of repression, usually exteriorized ones. The person seeks to repress ideas through activities in a social context. This tells us the harms of resistances. Every resistance reinforces the worldview according to which the truth is too dangerous to deal with. Resistances make the avoided problem seem worse. Moreover, as with any repressive pattern, once a resistance is habitual, the person is likely to utilize it in other contexts. As part of the patient's style of life, resistances deprive him of chances to develop and to overcome other kinds of problems. Resistances to the therapist's endeavor are almost always reproductions of the person's past ways of avoiding truth.

The proper handling of resistances may prove essential for this kind of therapy with some people, and not merely because they may hinder investigation. As controllable, harmful activities, resistances are a chief cause of the problem. Calling the patient's attention to them may have to become a regular occurrence. If the therapist asks, "How did you feel when your mother returned?" and the patient turns on the therapist in anger, there is much to be gained by considering the reaction more important than the answer to the original question. The reaction itself is almost surely harming him. Dropping that one resistance would give him more strength to consider the question asked—and many others like it. The answer to the question could come later, and might well prove unnecessary.

Interestingly, the psychoanalyst Wilhelm Reich caused a great stir in psychoanalysis when he presented the idea that one should bring up resistances early, as a kind of preface to Freudian treatment. As a psychoanalyst he could not appreciate the full importance of resistances. Nevertheless, he appreciated that the patient has some potential control over them, and he counted on the patient to surrender them. Our understanding bears out the preferability of his approach to Freud's on this important matter. Indeed, it tells us that Reich was accomplishing even more than his theory would have predicted when his patients dropped resistances.

The essentials of the method of therapy derive naturally

from what we know about pliancy. Just as psychoanalysis is based on the thesis that character structure determines behavior, our treatment method follows from the assumptions already presented and utilizes whatever observations were made proceeding from them. Belief in this point of view, at least the willingness to try it as a hypothesis, had to come first. Adherence to this new way of thinking leads to important discoveries. It also enables us to translate a series of conceptualizations out of the deterministic form in which they came, and into an organic one. With such concepts as symptom, repression, defense mechanism, resistance, seen organically, it is possible to see the real potentiality for change. In each case, we are led to study how some potentially controllable behavior is affecting the psyche. Time and again, conceptualizations that seemed beautiful but dead come to life almost magically.

The forms that this mode of psychotherapy may assume are various, reflecting the fact that there are an endless number of human personalities and of human relationships possible. Even people who seem to have the same outlook turn out to sustain it in somewhat different ways. Besides, patients differ in what they want of therapy, in their receptivity to new ideas, in the form and strength of their resistances, in their particular transference, in how desirous they are to talk about their past, and in countless other ways. What is invariant is the essential method of cure. Whatever the problem, the aim is to reveal the patient's hand in it and capacity for change. The therapist and patient work together to arrive at the significant discoveries, but only the patient can truly make use of them.

CHAPTER EIGHTEEN

Helping a Friend

Why do we have to accomplish our human lot? Because it is much to be here . . . and because they apparently need us, those things of the earth whose transience strangely concerns us.

Rainer Maria Rilke, The Ninth Duino Elegy

What's the best way for one person to help another with a psychological problem? When, if ever, is it possible? Psychology has offered virtually no advice on this important issue. Most psychologists seem indifferent to it. Indeed, many professionals actually warn against a layperson trying to help another person, intimating in one way or another that "you'll fail. You'll do more harm than good. You'll destroy the relationship." Were a distraught woman to say, "I think I can help my husband. I understand his problem. Please help me help him," the psychologist would have little or nothing to offer. The usual retort is, "Send him to a professional." Considering the current confusion within psychology over the issue of how one person helps another, to dismiss the possibility at this stage seems premature, if not smug.

Psychology has shirked the task of preparing the layman for a helping role partly because its determinism provides insufficient basis for offering a system a person could use to help another. As a result, current conceptualizations of therapy seem to demand too much of the helper—that he analyze, even take over, the other person's life. In reality, the heart of the contribution, apart from the friendship itself, is to help the friend to perceive and utilize his own capacity to help himself.

There is an allied reason for the neglect. Psychology is still struggling for identity. It has not yet established a set of principles and body of knowledge that would be agreed upon by all, or even a great majority of those within the profession. It's hard to know who the psychologist is and who the layman without recourse to school credentials. Even if suddenly accredited, few amateurs could pass for long as surgeons or certified public accountants or automobile mechanics. However, a terrifying number could pass as therapists and counselors, and many could doubtless do the job as well as or better than some now doing it with proper credentials. The distinction between amateur and professional has never been clear enough for the comfort of the profession. At this stage, psychology still has a strong need to "authenticate itself" as Thomas Szasz has put it; it has been far from secure enough to grant that amateurs can help people significantly, or to work at improving their skills even further.

There can be no hiding from this obligation on the part of psychology. With or without help, we who care most about each other, whatever our relationship, will stay up late into the night discussing each other's personal problems, or arguing about them and trying to accomplish what we can.

Any tendency on the part of the profession to disparage such efforts or take them lightly represents a disservice to people. True, there are some people who make a project out of helping others in order to avoid facing their own difficulties. But there are unsung heroes by the millions, toiling to pull someone out of despair, calling on the phone from work twice a day, willing to do anything to see a loved one happy, eager for information and help of any kind they can possibly get. Some of them spend a lifetime trying—out of commitment to higher values, loyalty, and not cowardice.

The pliancy point of view, and our work thus far, has an enormous amount to tell these people. Above all, it provides a way of looking at the person who is suffering, of seeing where his capacity for change may lie. It offers insights into the questions of whether one should try to help and under what conditions, as well as into how to preserve the necessary detachment and how to know when to quit because nothing of value is being accomplished. Most important, it suggests definite procedures that can be extremely useful, provided that both the helper and the helped agree to the project.

Interestingly, there is already a movement afoot to better enable people to help others. It began with the popularity and success of Alcoholics Anonymous. So-called "helper groups" of great diversity have formed, groups in which the members share some problem, like gambling or the impulse to batter their children. There are over 20 such groups, some with branches around the country or worldwide. The members are non-professionals who are convinced they can help each other and usually that the professions of psychology and psychiatry are unable to help people like them. They are sometimes referred to as the "anti-psychiatry movement," so manifestly different is their philosophy from that of current psychological thinking. Some are outspoken against its points of view; all are emphatic about the importance of people's choices. They believe in people's ability to overcome their problems by exerting will and making decisions that are healthy for them.

These groups work essentially in isolation, applying similar methods and finding them relatively successful, each group with its own particular problem. Thus, the findings themselves remain unconnected. Individual groups have not reached the generalizations that pooled knowledge would afford. Although they do not formulate a general theory like the theory of pliancy, they have arrived at important aspects of the point of view, instances of its application. Many of their conclusions are supported and thoroughly explained by the pliancy viewpoint. For instance, all dispute that the behavior in question is merely a "symptom," as psychoanalysis maintains. AA singled out this notion first, to disagree with it, asserting that alcoholism is a "progressive disease." To call the drinking a symptom, they say, plays into the idea that it is uncontrollable, a mere consequence, and makes it harder to appeal to the will. To view drinking as a symptom, with the implication that it need not be attacked, but will disappear when some underlying problem is resolved, is to overlook the fact that the indulgence itself makes the condition worse, causing it to progress. Gamblers Anonymous noted this about gambling, and so did other groups about their particular activity. Actually, because personality is organic, all psychological conditions, healthy ones as well as illnesses, are progressive. But ironically, because these various groups are each concerned with only a single condition and do not know this, they regard their particular problem as outside the general laws of psychology, which they think govern problems other than theirs.

Another discovery made by certain of these groups has been called the "helper-therapy principle." In simplest form it states that the person who works at helping another overcome a problem will profit as much or more than the one he is trying to help. Efforts at persuasion have their greatest effect on the persuader. As this principle was put in one of its applications:

A group in which criminal A joins with some noncriminals to change criminal B, is probably most effective in changing criminal A, not B.[59]

The persuader affects his own mind by his efforts. Our appreciation of the role of motive explains why. He adds to his own sense of self-worth. He reinforces his beliefs about the need to stay clear of the harmful practice and the possibility of succeeding in a new kind of life.

Helper groups have made other observations of the ways in which people's acts affect their minds, and even of the significance of their motivations. The groups, however, lacking a system of psychology to legitimize them, continue to feel their approach is unorthodox. A great many of their members have tried the usual forms of therapy, gone to professionals, and not been helped. If you visit any one of the groups, whether it is composed of drug addicts or people with claustrophobia or compulsive drinkers or compulsive gamblers, you would very likely be told that psychotherapy is notoriously unsuccessful for people with that particular problem. Of course, those helped with the problem by therapy never get to the particular groups, and one can only conjecture how many there are in comparison with those that fail. But it is telling that there is such distance between the work of these groups and that of formal psychology and that those within the profession seldom take interest in what these groups discover.

There is nothing "unpsychological" about what these groups have discovered, or about what they strive to accomplish. They are arriving at formulations and conclusions that are explicable by the theory of pliancy, and that enrich the theory with examples. It seems that almost wherever there is a large body of people trying to help themselves, the group has from the beginning stressed the importance of individuality, of choice, and of the consequences of acts. The theory of pliancy is the psychology that best integrates the findings of those groups. It accounts for many of these findings, showing them as instances of larger truths.

Most people's problems aren't so easily encapsulated. They can't simply look up their category in the reference book and find a group of others with the same problem. Not that the alcoholic's problem is so simple, but a salient feature of it is. In most cases, the nature of the problem isn't clear to begin with, only that there is a problem. The onlooker, the friend or person in love with the sufferer, may become aware of the difficulty first. And possibly has a real capacity to help. The challenge that confronts this person is what to do and how to do it.

For instance, a woman sees that her husband seldom lives up to his expectations and feels defeated. She has some insights into why. He's been on his present job for three years, and it's obvious from the conversations he reports that a newcomer is soon to be promoted over his head. His wife suspected it would happen. She witnessed him asking for reassurance too frequently, not listening enough, pressing people for answers, failing to recognize when people were uncomfortable—in short, acting insensitively. As onlooker she feels utterly alone. Millions find themselves in this position. They really have much to offer. But it is a matter of their knowing exactly what it is and how to offer it.

It has been argued that attempts to help do more harm than good. But this is simply another variant of the pessimism surrounding the whole project of personality change. That viewpoint overlooks the fact that people's problems often interfere with relationships, so that some of the problems encountered in the effort of one person helping another were there all along. In addition, the observation that people often fail to help others, instead of being seen as a reason for people not to try, ought to be a spur to psychology to equip people with insights so they could use their sensitivity more effectively.

Sometimes it has been argued that since the helper has a personal interest in the outcome, something to gain if the other person changes his behavior, he carries a disqualifying bias. However, standing to profit doesn't necessarily detract.

Nor does a bias in perception. Imperfect people can help one another; in fact, a bias can sometimes heighten one's sensitivity to just what another person needs. It's true that someone close by and emotionally concerned may find it harder than a professional therapist to tolerate failures, to stay back. This too must be dealt with, or the help might accomplish nothing. On the other hand, the deep concern that comes from wanting to share a life with a person helps one to withstand frustrations, so long as some plan is seen and there is at least some progress.

There's also a bias in *not* trying to help the person. Take the woman who watches her husband's decline, at great cost to both of them. If she does nothing, says nothing, it's as if she is cursed with her superior understanding. Unless she tries, she perhaps suffers from the bias of feeling convinced that her husband is hopeless, and that her only alternative is to contemplate life without him. Very likely, it is with this outlook that she has already chosen the dull existence of accepting him as he is. She has, by doing this, perpetuated and confirmed her belief that any effort on her part would be pointless, that people aren't really capable of changing. When this is so, broaching the subject to him would benefit her by helping to correct her bias.

Suppose that two people understand that decisions send messages to the mind. One or both has the knowledge of pliancy that shows what must be done to alter an outlook. Some timely insight, the recognition of a pattern, a well-posed question, could save considerable time. Most people want to limit the assistance they seek from others anyhow, and it is best to do as much of the work oneself as possible.

There are some people whose curiosity and trust invite them to enjoy the adventure of working together as a team. It might be just at one stage—at identifying the problem, for instance, spotting the tendency. There's certainly some risk of the project's causing trouble or bringing trouble to a head if it's already there. For instance, if the "helper" is basically dissatisfied with himself and is using the role to cover up his dissatisfaction and express anger, the prognosis is poor. How is one to tell? There need to be safeguards against such an imbalance, ways of discovering it at any rate, and stopping the project.

A man experiences his aging without money or personal distinction as a profound defeat. His wife looks elderly to him, for which he cannot forgive her. He insists that she never reveal her age, that she dress almost ludicrously youthfully; he winces if she assumes a maternal role with other people, and later disparages them to her in order to prevent a recurrence of this reminder that his life is a failure. His very mistreatment of her actually reinforces his feeling that he is a failure.

Such relationships are only too common. For our purposes it should be absolutely understood that either person has the right to stop at any time. If the critic can't stop, or resents having to pass a week without pointing out the supposed tragic flaw, almost surely he is responding to some compulsive need, likely to be dangerous. Probably, it's nearly always best that the joint effort be discontinued, at least for a while. Right or wrong, it's important that the one being helped can ask the helper to drop the project entirely so that the relationship can return to its previous basis.

It might be the helper who needs this privilege. For instance, the person receiving the help unexpectedly turns on him in rage and says spiteful things. The next day the person expects him to resume his role as if nothing happened. Perhaps this would be tolerable once or twice. But a lifetime of being used as sympathetic advisor and then berated for interfering is demoralizing. The right to stop helps both persons preserve their sense of dignity.

Besides, attempting to stop is the best way of diagnosing misuses of the role of helper and of heading off bigger trouble. The person who can't stop giving the help is almost certainly responding to some profound need of his own and is caught up in compulsive behavior. This means that at certain times giving the aid feels more important to him than the relationship itself. At such times he is likely to be insufficiently concerned with how the recipient feels, or even with whether he improves. The recipient may not be fully aware that this is so, that the help is compulsive, but comes to fear the advice.

In the following case, a boy did not appreciate that his father was giving him advice irrationally and compulsively. But he felt the abuse of the help. The father was a highly pedantic man. He never struck the boy but talked to him laceratingly, using psychological terms to describe what was "wrong" with him, and criticizing him under the guise of being constructive. One day when walking through the park with his father, the boy said casually in response to some criticism, "Today I don't want to improve myself in any way. Let's just talk." The father fell silent. A little later, he launched another intellectual attack on the boy, who repeated his request. Unexpectedly, the father burst into a fury, sputtered and became red faced, and for the first time he struck his son, a blow across the face with his open hand. Who knows what the father's "constructive" criticisms had meant to him?

Ideally, the helper should not consider himself to be superior to the person receiving the help. This means that he could readily change roles and see nothing humiliating in discussing some failing of his own with the other person. If the imbalance is always in one direction, the same person constantly helping the other, it may be that the helper has a problem about revealing his own weakness. This might come out in the form of high-handedness or pity toward the other person, thereby hindering their work. It's not just the one being helped who needs a good attitude toward mistakes.

Arrangements in which two people help one another on separate problems are sometimes practical. A helper's reluctance to take the opposite role may suggest that as helper the person might feel superior and not have the most favorable motives. The important thing, however, is that the people psychologically *could* reverse roles, not that they do. "I'll help you if you help me" is not an arrangement between friends but a barter for services, and the spirit of this work, the way it is done and why, is very much a part of it.

CHAPTER NINETEEN
Parenthood

Everyone knows that children are impressionable. Certain actions by adults seriously influence the child's perceptions and expectations of himself. But what is the exact relation between the child's social experiences and his future development? For parents to grasp this is to see more sharply where to make their efforts and also to see what they cannot do. Our understanding of pliancy gives us sharp insight into how parents can contribute to the child's developing psyche.

Too often the impressionability of childhood has been construed mechanistically, as if parents could somehow transmit values and an outlook to an essentially receptive child. According to this view, the child is impressionable for a short interval during which parents should bestow love, attention and understanding so that the child can emerge with a sense of self-worth. Failures, any kind of neglect during this crucial period, might cause the child to have low self-esteem later on. We see this view amplified in psychoanalysis, although it did not originate there. It assumes that a well-imparted impression will last. Indeed, the measure of how serious an impact events had on a child is how durably they affect his personality. If the impact seems to last, then the impression must have been powerful. This idea encapsulates the position. It makes parental behavior during this period analogous to writing with indelible ink.

The impressionability thesis put enormous pressure on parents who held it, inhibiting millions. Making matters worse has been that there were few prescriptions for the right kinds of behavior. It was asserted that adults often show the dire effects of being neglected when they were children, but there was no clear definition of neglect. Nor has there been any way of telling in advance how harmful some occurrence, like divorce of the parents, would be. It might prove to have a powerful impact, but one could only wait and see.

The impressionability thesis led many parents to do too much and blame themselves for decisions they'd made. It was as if they'd somehow stamped bad attitudes onto their children, cheated them. Not appreciating that the child's decisions are the necessary and immediate causes of his outlook, they have failed to see what they might have done and where intervention might have helped. And because they have not realized that an outlook becomes renewed continually, they have been unable to see the contributions they might still make.

Many parents respond with a kind of psychological absenteeism. It wasn't that they wanted to shirk parenthood, although this was sometimes the case. But since so many kinds of errors could be harmful, the safest approach has seemed to be to avoid making demands that might cause the child displeasure and a sense of injury. This point of view entered psychology; it seemed to say that the wise and loving parent will foster a healthy child without close scrutiny but merely by having the right attitudes, and that most parental failings are due to faults of action instead of inaction. Often the child was left without boundaries, and did not learn the enormous rewards of disciplined striving—namely, a sense of self and belief in the meaningfulness of what is striven for. Permissiveness came to imply the abandonment not just of procedures but also of values for the child. It reached the point of many parents not even wanting to acknowledge a plan for what their children would become. There are even some experts who, in reacting to the ill effects of tampering with children's lives, concluded that parents should set no goals whatever.

> It would be extremely presumptuous on my part to tell you what kind of a child you should have, or what kind of a person you should want your child to grow up to be. That's why some of you have gotten tired of the books on how to raise children. Because the books proceed as if there were a model person to strive for, and if you just do this and that you will get such a person.[8]

But of course parents will always have desires for their children, ideals in mind for what they are to become—as much as for themselves, or even more so, sometimes, if they have given up on themselves. In fact, parents are often best able to articulate their own ideals by saying what they want their child to be like. True, when the parent has certain expectations of the child—that the child love sports or choose a particular career, for example—there can be trouble. But as for qualities, the child's emotional instrument, this is something different. Virtually all parents, if they reflected, would claim many traits for their children. And in various ways a child can acquire any of them. They do not limit the child, but rather enable the child to make sensitive and passionate choices.

Included are a sense of self-worth, spontaneity, curiosity, independence, courage, stability, and the capacity to experience a wide range of emotions. In addition, most parents would, if they thought about it, want their children to be able to romanticize life as opposed to becoming cynical, to listen to others, to take criticism well, and to be able to profit from mistakes. Obviously, parents cannot protect their children entirely from loneliness any more than from fear of death. More likely, the child protects the parent from both, the parent for the first time thinking of his own death as less significant than that of another human being. But the aim is to have children live deeply and without neurosis, for them to know while they live that, as Rilke said, "It is much to be here."

Parents must become aware of desirable traits—know what they are and have a sense of when the child is creating them. At the heart of the matter are the impressions of self and of existence that the child acts upon. The child, of course, does not reflect on his worldview and cannot see that he is creating himself while striving for tangible rewards. But the parent can know this. This in itself defines the obligation of parenthood. The child, by decisions, prolongs certain impressions and creates capacities, enlarging some and diminishing others. The parent, in a position to see and know what the child cannot, can make particular decisions feasible. By "parent," I mean anyone who fulfills that role in the child's life.

The study of pliancy reveals certain things that parents cannot do, as well as a whole domain over which they can make their influence felt. Parents, first of all, have enormous influence on what the child finds to experiment with. The aim is to create a home where a healthy state of mind is successful for the child—that is, where the child finds pleasure in acts that reinforce a favorable view of himself and life. Does music play in the home? Is there kindness for the child to see? Do people touch one another? The child will form impressions based on what is seen, using trial and error.

In constructing the home environment, parents can also take into account facts of temperament that make particular decisions easier for some children than others. Differences can be seen almost from birth. Some children are inclined to be placid, others irritable; children differ in sociability and in how well they tolerate frustration. These differences do not ultimately limit the child or determine values or the adult outlook. But acts easy for one child might seem much more difficult to another with a different temperament. Parents can take such differences into account.

The study of pliancy tells the parent to watch the premises the child is acting upon. The child will retain conclusions only by habitually renewing them. Parents can influence this process, at least much of the time, by understanding how it occurs. For the parent to formulate, "What might I do to help the child?" it is necessary first to ask, "What might the child do that would create the best outlook?"

A girl of eight, for example, had reason to become fearful. It had been a nightmarish year; her mother had been in an auto accident and remained in a coma. The girl was parcelled out to aunts and uncles, whose comings and goings were enigmatic to her. She was removed from her friends and sent to a different school, although it was not very far away. During much of that year she saw people whispering about her mother, there seemed a mystery with a horrible solution—but they simply told her that her mother would be fine.

Now her mother had mostly recovered and the family was back together. But the girl had unquestionably suffered anguish over a whole year, been more profoundly hurt than most children are. She seemed to have quit on life, to have lost interest in everything. To help this girl recover, it becomes important to appreciate the role of her behavior, of choices still to come. It is important to see not just impressions formed, though they are important, but impressions she is already acting upon, which sustain the harm. If there is to be lasting injury, it must be that the girl herself sustains it by decisions to come. Despite the real improvements in her present life, a mode of behavior might survive, one that would keep her feeling that things are still bad. Although it is, of course, helpful to offer the child a stable home and give assurances, the problem parents face is to discover these harmful decisions before they become a habit of mind that grows, becoming more difficult to replace.

Which of her many activities, especially newly adopted ones, are causing the child to continue to believe that things will not work out, thus renewing her worst expectations? This is the critical question. While shuffling from home to home the girl made an obvious retreat. Now she disparages herself, restrains enthusiasm, shies away from making friends; she shows no ambition at school, although she once cared a great deal and was an early reader. The parent who has already formulated the idea that the girl needs predictability and a stable home has worried too much about simply providing it. The pitfall is for parents to spend full effort proving to the child that the home is stable, that they are loving, without asking anything of the child. The girl will need to act, to change her mode and trust relationships, to trust her abilities if her present outlook is to change. It is especially important for the parents to identify any refusal of hers to commit herself to friends or work because such decisions renew her sense that there will be no tomorrow that she can count on.

Of course, if treated well and given assurances about life, the girl might be inclined to take more chances. Especially if she were talented or attractive, and people responded well to her, she might drop some of her reserve. But this might not occur in more than a limited way. With her parents trying to make up for lost love, she might still hold back in places, refuse to invest in relationships in her future.

Much more to the point would be for the parents while giving her love to prevail upon her to contact friends, to share experiences, to do anything that would replace her crestfallen conception of relationships. Firmer discipline, encouragement that success in school really matters, might motivate her to act in ways that could prove to her the future was stable. Although her parents cannot give her self-love, they can present the idea of her being worthwhile and show her how to create this sense. And they can see whether she is taking up the cues.

There's no need to pinpoint the child's exact worldview in order to be helpful. A parent knowing nothing about pliancy might have said, in response to the child's asking for advice about calling a friend, "Why not?" And suppose the child answered, "She might not want to see me." One could imagine the parent replying, "You'll live. Besides, the more you put into things, the more you get out of them." Sensitive parents could help a child this way, without knowing exactly how the help was being given but cognizant of the child's want to do something and fear of doing it. But it seems even better to have a conscious sense of the process, which shows how such help can be regularly given.

Naturally, one can't always know the child's motivations, although the child may be only some minutes away from talking about them. Nor is mind reading advisable, telling the child "what you really think." One can easily be wrong and even more important, successful mind reading deprives the child of the chance to identify experiences and report them. Some of the most seemingly paralyzed children are those whose parents—being real or amateur psychologists—flood them with interpretations and statements about what they must feel. On the other hand, children often readily report why they do things; what they want to accomplish. Often it isn't more than five minutes conversation away from the child's saying frankly that he feels inadequate, if a sore point is touched.

Parents can profit by attention to the child's behavior in innumerable ways. Take the child's reaction to failure. Much has been said about protecting the child from the experience. If, however, the child can handle it—try again or at least admit that things went wrong and seek after reasons why they did—then the whole experience may be invaluable. How can one learn to cope with failure without having experienced it? The real problem of repeated failure, especially if it is humiliating, is that the child may come to adopt defensive modes of behavior, forms of not trying again, which keep alive the sense of himself as incompetent.

Of special importance are patterns of behavior based on fear, which are attempts to deny or hide the truth. At first, the aim may be to delude others, but it is most convenient to avoid such prickly realities oneself. Bragging and lying, as a rule, stem from fear, and a sense that the truth would not be good enough. The child who habitually lies or invents some fraud to conceal weakness or get attention is a child under enormous pressure. As our analysis showed earlier, not just fear but these very habits of denial are the source of repression and neurosis. Parents who know this can do much to discourage them. A positive momentum is under way when the child expresses traits thought desirable, such as curiosity and independence. It is not simply the act that matters. One can virtually constrain the child to act in certain ways by the use of heavy rewards and punishments, but here it is the intention behind the act we're concentrating on. Despite their almost unlimited monarchy, no parent can commandeer the child's intentioned act. On the other hand, by noting desirable acts, moments of the child's loyalty or perseverence or truthfulness, a parent can provide opportunity for more such moments. Commending an act has the risk of possibly changing its purpose, but as a rule the additional motive, to please the parent, merely accompanies the other and does not dislodge it.

With children especially, it is often a matter of seeing where the fancy lights, where moments of the trait lie, and encouraging these. Carson McCullers wrote a short story about a man who learned to love by starting with a rock that appealed to him, then going on to feel deeply about a tree and finally a cloud, the most transitory. It was not a particular act or object that was crucial, but that a certain view and feeling underlay the behavior.

The same in evaluating education: generalizations should not be made solely from what the child has learned but from what the child strives for. The language student who learns a thousand vocabulary words for an exam but develops no love of the language or curiosity about it is almost sure to stop. The one who learns less but with a good feeling about the subject will far outstrip him. It is important for parents to think in terms of the momentum behind any of the child's ways of thinking. If there is any predictability about the future, at least the near future, it lies in the study of this momentum.

All this talks about how the parent can get the child started in the right direction. Something more can be done, or at least striven for. Eventually, the child might learn to make the analyses, to consider how choices might be affecting his own outlook, and to be guided by some answers. The child with good attitudes, confirming them every day in behavior, is in a good position to elaborate on this outlook. It may feel firm already—say, the desire to learn, the honesty, optimism. But there are to be challenges, when the parent is no longer there, temptations to act in ways that feel comfortable but would erode the outlook. And there are times, when things have gone wrong, when self-analysis becomes absolutely necessary. Ultimately, the aim must be to impart the needed information so that the child, or young adult, can consider how choices affect his own mind. Such knowledge can give the needed flexibility, and can be the crowning feature of real independence.

Many lessons lie along the road toward understanding. In the early years, the child must evolve the idea of a self that initiates actions. He makes this discovery mostly alone, later greatly clarifying it by language, which has words for "I" and "me." The parent reaffirms the notion that the child's choices are causal, looking mainly at the child's well-being or safety as a consequence. This is important—and comprehensible—information for the child.

But the child can also learn that choices and whole habits affect his view of himself. Gradually, the child can learn that you produce confidence by doing a thing well, that habitual behavior is easier, that lying can make a person feel far away from loved ones, alone and frightened. Doing something new can be frightening but also exciting.

The child must not only learn that acts affect the spirit, but also must come to value the inner life, to consider his own hopefulness and view of himself as worth sacrificing for. That consciousness is a wonderful opportunity can be shown by teaching the child to make sacrifices to improve its quality. The very taking it into account, making decisions for their effect on the inner life, affirms its importance.

The ultimate stage is to impart the facts of pliancy so far as one believes them or knows them. What you do affects your outlook in a definite way. Sometimes an intelligent ten-year-old can grasp the essentials, but as with the answer to any question, the child should be allowed to take any part of it, not necessarily all of it at once. This gives the child a way to make important decisions, one that might not be used for many years but might prove invaluable later on.

Maturational stages, so far as they concern body development, play a role in the child's capacities. But the problem is always to use these capacities constructively, whatever they are. One child tries to be less demanding of others for the sake of friendship. Another battles his urge to get up and run around when a friend is talking, and a third musters the courage to step forward and extend a hand when introduced to his cousin. All three might by their acts be emphasizing in their own minds, "The company of others is worth making sacrifices for." Developmental changes in the early years might determine which acts are easy, which the challenges. The challenges, however, are always there, and the true construction comes out of the person's way of meeting them, dealing with them or shirking them.

CHAPTER TWENTY
Science and Psychology

Any form of psychology resting on the acceptance of consciousness and will might seem easy prey to the charge of being unscientific. There are three cornerstones of science —verifiability, the ability to predict, and the ability to control events. The argument goes that any subjective system like ours, in assuming human freedom, fails miserably on all three counts.

Within the field of psychology, it has often been taken for granted that its members must fall into either of two camps. In one are these self-styled scientists, who would approach problems of the mind using essentially the methods developed to study events in which mind plays no part, methods that have previously produced success in the physics or chemistry laboratory. These people would deny that there could be any use changing the basic methods of investigation to study human beings. They range from being skeptical of the work done by us (we being subjectivists who believe in will) to being downright contemptuous of it. Many seem to believe that we have forfeited all claim to verifiability along with all hope of being able to predict and control events because of the assumptions we make.

It is sometimes even assumed that we perhaps don't understand the values of verifiability or of predictability and control. Or that we simply don't have the discipline of mind to think their way. In their view, the work of mentalists like myself is either meaningless or will someday be explained by their principles.

Science has shone a great searchlight on the universe. But the trouble with so bright a light is that those standing beyond it become indistinguishable. It does not follow automatically that the person who studies mental events has no interest in verification and wants dispensation from the need for it. Such an attitude results in the likening of all subjectivists to one another and to mystics, as if those who studied mental processes were by nature indifferent to the demonstrability of anything. In this respect, the scientific group sometimes treats us like harmless village idiots.

The accusation that we are indifferent to scientific criteria has been a serious mistake in the case of many of us. I, for one, have always retained a lively belief in the value of verifiability, and have never doubted the ability to predict and control events as the criterion of knowledge. I am not proud of the fact that I cannot apply such criteria in their usual form in my work. Rather, I do not construe this difficulty as sufficient reason to abandon psychology in the old sense.

Speaking for at least some of us, it is not that we love verifiability, predictability, and control less than the "hard scientist" does, but that we cherish the study of consciousness more. Many of us have felt from childhood an absorption with the human mind. We will not now turn our backs on what interests us most because other kinds of events are more easily verifiable. We cannot satisfy the quest merely by drawing effortless conclusions about unimportant events. We see ourselves as flying with imperfect instruments. But our decision to study the mental process is a flight we think well worth taking.

Nor are these researchers who work in the laboratory the only ones who imagine that the assumption of human freedom invalidates the possibility of prediction and control. There are highly sympathetic clinicians, eager to take the journey with us, nonetheless convinced that we have surrendered the possibility of ever satisfying the basic criteria. One of them wrote not long ago:

> What confounds the aims of prediction and control above all is our freedom. In those areas of behavior popularly considered voluntary, we are free not to be predicted and controlled. . . . It seems that if psychologists are to survive scientifically, they must abandon the futile aims of prediction and control.[51]

Some of those who cling to their belief in volition feel that they do so at the expense of having to surrender predictability.

But scientific method, although it applies when studying purely reactive material, has a serious flaw when applied to research with humans as subjects. The logic behind the method as it is applied in the laboratory presupposes a distinction. The material studied is assumed to be merely reactive, not to have a will of its own, and it's assumed that the experimenter has a will of his own, which he exercises in applying his procedure. This distinction presents no problem to the chemist. He freely subjects his material to new procedures, and his subject matter merely reacts. This is implicit in the notion that the experimenter controls the so-called independent variable, and the responses of the subject matter comprise dependent variables.

The experimental psychologist working with animals makes the same distinction, implicitly. He is free; his animals respond to the way he treats them. He rewards the animal voluntarily. All this is necessary, his seeing himself as the one to employ the independent variable, for him to conclude that his procedure affected the animal in some meaningful way. There seems some loss in this, but one can't prove it. No one ever had direct access to a dog's mind.

But there is a stupendous contradiction in the logic of this kind of experimentation where human beings are subjects. The same creature exactly is doing the experiment as the one being studied. Whatever human nature is, it applies to both. The experimenter, however, assumes that he himself is free, his acts are voluntary, and that the acts of those other human beings now serving as subjects are not free. Or to look at this contradiction another way, the same person assumes that he is free when serving as experimenter, and then, an hour later if he serves as subject for someone else, it is assumed he is not free. This contradiction is glossed over. But a view about human nature, in this case the mechanistic one, can hardly be called coherent if it requires holding two contradictory views of human nature at the same time.

Scientific method was, after all, designed for a nonsubjective universe, one without choice. It is not surprising that when carried over in unchanged form and applied to human beings, it generates such a contradiction. Its whole direction is off-center for the highest purposes of psychology. This inner contradiction amounts to more than just a quirk to be passed over. It is a consequence of the attempt to view human beings as mere respondents, and is an exact counterpart of the trouble that therapists have whose system makes deterministic assumptions about their patients.

And, before acknowledging our relative impoverishment as far as predicting and controlling events is concerned, it should be noted that psychology has thus far done very little of what it promises in that regard. From the standpoint of affording us discoveries we can use in our lives, predictable truths, psychological research has been an abysmal provider from the beginning. Psychotherapists just about never turn to reports of experiments to help them. Most would consider it laughable to examine the results of experiments for insights. Nor would researchers expect them to. There is hardly a truth in all of psychology that has been uncovered experimentally and is now employed by people practically. Many psychologists are aware of this failing. They blame it on the complexities of their subject matter, maintaining that there are too many variables to control. Researchers attempt to get around the difficulty by the use of giant samples. Slight effects in people are more detectable statistically in large groups than in individuals. If even a small change of attitude occurs in some small fraction of people treated in some particular way, then the experimenter feels warranted in concluding that the procedure he studied has "some effect." However, conclusions drawn from slight differences between groups have virtually no applicability to the single case.

Applied mathematicians have worked to develop statistical procedures to pinpoint lesser and lesser effects. New and more intricate methods of making comparisons always seem to be coming along. Many researchers, if not most, spend a lifetime employing techniques that are too advanced mathematically for them to handle. There is always a sense that with some slightly more powerful tool, they can pinpoint something truly important.

Why has psychological experimentation failed to uncover principles or to give us important truths regarding how attitudes form? It never seems to address itself to the questions that matter to us. It isn't a matter of refining methods of measurement. The answer is that the methods of science have not yet been properly adapted to work with humans. In the name of science, psychologists have been content to do nothing more than seize the logic and methods of study used on inorganic matter, which, indeed, merely reacts.

Looking at the usual version of scientific method, the controlled experiment done with humans as subjects, we see that it is entirely geared for measuring the effects of an experimenter's procedure, and each phase is carried out with this in mind. The psychological experimenter chooses his subjects and assigns them to different groups, which he then treats differently. It would be unthinkable for the subjects

228 THE PLIANT ANIMAL

to determine by their behavior which group they go into. He draws his inferences on the assumption that his subjects merely respond and do not initiate behavior. He conceives of a deterministic chain between his input and their responses. For instance, he shows a film to fourth-grade children and then studies their emotional reactions or behavior. Which children see the film and which don't is up to him. His purpose is to determine how the film affects them, and, ultimately, others like them. Observe the close analogy to the kind of experiment a chemist might carry out.

However, this enables the psychologist to discover only those effects on people caused by forces on them from without, and gives him no possibility of identifying how people affect themselves by their voluntary actions. Such an approach was fine when inanimate objects were studied—they are well-behaved; they simply react to what is done to them. The main influence on our attitudes, however, is the one we exert on them by our own choices. The usual controlled experiment permits the researcher no way of studying this influence.

There has been a growing sense that something is basically wrong with traditional psychological experimentation, mirroring a growing discontent with deterministic psychology. This sense has not been focused, but is sometimes expressed as concern for the person who serves as subject in such an experiment. Some in the profession consider many experiments to be dehumanizing to the subjects. They have begun to suggest that the very conducting of certain experiments has been unfair. This unrest is to be found in some interesting comments written recently into the American Psychological Association's standards on ethical principles to be observed when experiments are done with people.

> Steps are taken to insure that the student is treated with respect and courtesy. In the service of this concept, the term "subject" has been abandoned in some universities and the expression "research participant" has replaced it.

"Research participant" does indeed show more appreciation of the person's role as initiator than "subject." The person is participating instead of being subjected to the experimenter's procedure. But what has been recognized as imperfect language really reflects something very much bigger, a whole view of people as respondents, implicit in the very design of the typical experiment.

Actually, rather than lead to chaos, the system that follows from our axioms, the foundation on which the theory of pliancy rests, provides a very useful ability to predict and control. The key to seeing this is to realize that the main challenges are not predicting or controlling another person's behavior, as the scientist does in the laboratory, but of being able to produce desirable effects in ourselves—effects that we can anticipate. Indeed, the very purpose of this book has been to show that certain mental occurrences are predictable and controllable. It is valuable to see exactly the kind of predictability and control our system affords. Every discovery of a relationship between a voluntary act and an outcome enhances this ability to predict and control.

As for verifiability, we cannot see each other's minds at work. But the *principles* that relate choices to their effects are verifiable, often easily so. Take the observation that if you force yourself to stop a habitual activity, the urge for it increases at first. Or that during this period, there is heightened consciousness of the need. Or the statement that there are peaks, but if you go on resisting the urge, it diminishes. Every living human has observed such effects, and can produce them.

In such cases the person is manipulating his own voluntary behavior and observing inevitable changes in what is involuntary. Instead of an experimenter systematically producing some impact on an organism or inanimate object in his laboratory, this is the case of a person controlling input into the part of him that is "inanimate" in the sense of being respondent only. The predictability of this simple effect of breaking a habit is stronger than that of many phenomena thought to be demonstrated in the laboratory. It would be hard for the experimental psychologist to uncover any relationship even approaching it in regularity of occurrence. Hundreds of examples of this kind of causation have been given in this book, some more complex and less precisely predictable than this, but all verifiable and predictable. Indeed, the whole study of pliancy investigates a kind of inevitability—that between act and inner consequence. As psychology becomes the study of such inevitability, which it must if it is ever to fulfill its promise, it must convert the notions of predictability and control and use them in this way. This viewpoint allows for the coexistence of freedom and the possibility of producing predictable effects in our psychic lives.

Apparently, the theologian Paul Tillich held this viewpoint when he wrote: "Man has freedom not in the sense of indeterminacy, but in the sense of being able to determine himself through decisions in the center of his being."

In certain experiments, this has been approached. The experimenter seems at the brink of considering his subjects to be acting voluntarily. Indeed, such experiments hold special fascination because they seem to cry out for the analysis we have done in this book. Still, the experimenter, constrained to think of his input as the cause and hesitant to think in other ways, misses the possibility, or at least does not state it.

I have in mind a number of exciting experiments done by social psychologists, especially in connection with Leon Festinger's concept of "cognitive dissonance." In one, for instance, Festinger and an associate, J. Merrill Carlsmith, had college students perform some tedious tasks, such as packing small items. Afterwards, the experimenters divided the students into two groups. One group was paid $20 to lie to a new batch of students, telling them that the task was interesting. The other group was paid only $1 to do the same thing. Students who lied for the $20 continued to feel the task was dull, but those paid only a dollar tended to feel less that way, to *believe* their lie. The experimenters interpreted their findings wholly in terms of their own input—the difference between amounts of money offered. From this and from some similar experiments, they concluded that lesser rewards change people more than big rewards do.

From our point of view, the voluntary striving for $20 had a different effect on the subjects than when money was not the crucial issue. Appreciating that voluntary acts affect people, we too reached the conclusion that the size of rewards matters. But only indirectly, if one seeks them. Which truly produced the change—the rewards or the subjects' striving for them? Practically, the answer makes all the difference, since if it is the rewards themselves, then the experimenter produced the change. But if it is the striving, then a person, knowing this, can resist a harmful change in himself, no matter what reward system confronts him.

Looking at this same experiment from our point of view, we consider the students' decision to comply or not as voluntary, and think of this behavior as the cause. We may think of the students as grouping themselves by what they did. For us, an important contrast is between the group that complied and the one that did not. The students who did not comply thus come into the picture. A study of those who refused to lie even for $20 might show that they too changed themselves. At least some of them would intensify their belief in the truth and in the need to tell it, in its value. Those who merely resisted a dollar, we would predict, would not do this to the same extent. The point is that such an experiment might be done and interpreted from the standpoint that the subjects affected themselves. Although it may not seem so at first, it is quite possible to study people's decisions as voluntary, and to draw firm conclusions, statistically sound, regarding their effects.

Suppose, to consider an experiment that might be designed for this purpose, that a thousand alcoholics who enter a clinic over some time period have all vowed to stop drinking, and that during the next two years a certain number stick to their vow and the rest do not. The usual method is to look for prognosticators of who will stop drinking, cues that might have been interpreted as signifying this at the start. And this has real value. A more effective method, however, would be to compare a sample of those who stopped with those who continued, to see the effects that stopping had on their personality. Of course, controls would be necessary. Comparisons must be made between people who, on personality measures, were similar to start with. Observe that the subjects have classified themselves into one of two groups by their decisions. They control the independent variable. We are measuring the effects on them, on their personalities, of how they exercise that control.

Many questions might be answered by this method. What about the abstainer's attitudes toward other things? Toward the value of work? Toward the possibility of friendship? Of love? Toward the decency of people? What about their optimism about the future of the world? One could go on and on, identifying such effects of their behavior on them. And one could measure these effects, often pinpointing them with instruments no better than those used today and blamed for failures of experimentation.

Naturally, people respond to incentives. But experimental psychology must encompass more than the mere study of how they do. The study of how their own choices affect people, of the very laws of pliancy, is far more important. Research, if it proceeded along these lines, would soon yield a body of highly verifiable knowledge. Its findings would be practical beyond anything psychology has yet given us.

For psychology to leave its infancy, it must be bold enough to set its own direction. No longer a science *manqué*, psychology must fully declare itself as the study of events not so readily measurable as external physical occurrences but every bit as important.

CHAPTER TWENTY-ONE

In Conclusion

Far from being a creature who cannot change, the human being has incredible pliancy.

To study sameness with the intention of classifying people as like or unlike one another is to set one's sights on seeing how we do not change. Yet this is essentially what psychology has done. It has emphasized the discovery of traits, especially those beginning in early childhood and lasting a long time. This emphasis on constancy has precluded psychology from seeing the real faculty human beings have to control their vision of life.

The adaptations that we have made as a result of our wondrous pliancy show the need for a new emphasis. There is as much room for a discipline that studies the potentiality for change as there is for the one now investigating sameness. Changes in our nature have characteristically been made without being planned. We often alter our outlooks as a result of new dedication on our part, sometimes suggested by new necessities. Not that circumstances themselves have ever been sufficient to alter character. It has been our methods of coping with them that have, most immediately, produced the change. The study of pliancy, of how we adapt and orient ourselves, is the direct method of understanding how to employ this faculty, which now is exercised almost always unconsciously.

Startlingly little attention has been given to studying this possibility. Every psychologist thinks about freedom and the limitations of its use. But to push back the frontier of learning requires a radical restatement of the givens. What I have tried to show is that by pursuing particular axioms, psychology might fulfill this purpose. It can systematically proceed to discover the principles that account for human pliancy. What has, in our ancestors, been an unconsidered consequence of decisions, the individual psyche, may be constructed more deliberately. Decisions can be made for the sake of producing an outlook. In this way, voluntary power may be used for one's own sake, not simply to elicit better reactions from others. The creation of self-esteem can be internal and direct.

Therefore, the most important question a person can ask is: *How do my own actions affect me?* The study of pliancy is designed to answer particular versions of this question by comprehending the whole process, to harness the power of our own adaptability for our conscious use.

I've talked about a potentiality and a way of studying it. That is far more important, in my opinion, than any particular conclusion reached, which the reader might dispute, or which might turn out to be only one small instance of a general law as yet to be discovered. The aim, above all, has been to suggest the fruitfulness of this kind of study. If even a small fraction of those in the profession gave it serious attention, think how much more we could know about the process before long.

Consider the alternatives. Suppose this book has been based on assumptions entirely false. The human being is not capable of voluntary acts, or if there is such an ability, these acts do not reach deeply enough inside a person to change his outlook in a meaningful way. It would follow that our character is our fate and we cannot regulate it or control it. If so, then the usual psychology, which only studies the forces brought to bear on us and their effects, would be accurate. However, our comprehension of this psychology would be ultimately unimportant. There is no suggestion that we possess the power to use any knowledge about ourselves for the sake of change. Our helplessness would indeed be a tragedy. There would be hardly a difference between looking forward in life and looking back. In either case we would see nothing but a fatalistic chain.

This, however, would be nothing in comparison to the tragedy that would be ours if the alternative is true. Suppose human beings are actually creatures of choice, bearing power over their psychic destiny, but they refuse to study this possibility because of the desire to liken themselves to machines. Human beings, possessing the ability to change their whole outlook on life, would, out of loyalty to a theory, have deprived themselves of seeing this possibility and would have no system revealing what they might do for themselves. Given a full chance at redemption, we would have concluded that there is no possibility. Our psychology would indeed be a blindfold.

No irony could match the size of this one. Our possibility of repossessing not just ourselves but society would have been forfeited. It seems that we have no reasonable choice but to try the only place where there might be a door. Human possibility seems equated with the investigation of pliancy and the discovery of how to harness this power of adaptability that resides within all of us.

References

1. Allport, George, "Reply to Bertocci." *Psychological Review*, 47, 501–532, 1940.

2. Allport, Gordon W. *Personality and Social Encounter: Selected Essays*. Boston: Beacon Press, 1960.

3. Ardrey, Robert. *The Territorial Imperative*. New York: Atheneum, 1966.

4. Bannister, D. *Issues and Approaches in the Psychological Therapies*. London: Wiley, 1975.

5. Beach, Frank. "The Descent of Instinct." *Psychological Review*, 62, 401–410, 1940.

6. Benedict, Ruth. *Patterns of Culture*. Boston: Houghton Mifflin, 1961.

7. Bergin, Alan & Suinn, R. "Individual Psychotherapy and Behavior Therapy." *Annual Review of Psychology*, 540, 1975.

8. Bettleheim, Bruno. *Dialogues with Mothers*. New York: Avon, 1978.

9. Breland, Keller and Breland, Marian. "The Misbehavior of Organisms." *Animal Behavior*, 455–460. New York: Holt, Rinehart and Winston, 1965.

10. Darwin, Charles Robert. *The Expression of the Emotions in Man and Animals*. Westport, Connecticut: Greenwood Press, 1969.

11. Dostoevski, Fedor M. *Memoirs from the House of the Dead*. New York: Oxford University Press, 1965.

12. Dunlap, Knight. *Habits: Their Making and Unmaking*. New York: Liveright, 1949.

13. Eccles, Sir John Carew. *The Brain and the Unity of Conscious Experience*. Cambridge: University Press, 1965.

14. Eddington, Sir Arthur Stanley. *Science and the Unseen World*. Folcraft, Pennsylvania: Folcraft Press, 1979.

15. Efron, Robert. "Biology Without Consciousness—and Its Consequences." *Perspectives in Biology and Medicine*, 11, 1967.

16. Efron, Robert. "The Conditioned Reflex: A Meaningless Concept." *Perspectives in Biology and Medicine*, 9, 1966.

17. Eysenck, Hans Jurgen. *Experiments in Behavior Therapy*. New York: Macmillan, 1964.

18. Festinger, Leon. *A Theory of Cognitive Dissonance*. Stanford: University Press, 1957.

19. Festinger, Leon and Carlsmith, J. "Cognitive Consequences of Forced Compliance." From Aronson, Elliot. *The Social Animal*. San Francisco: W. H. Freeman, 1976.

20. Freud, Anna. *The Ego and the Mechanisms of Defence*. Translated by Cecil Barnes. London: Hogarth Press, 1948.

21. Freud, Sigmund. *Beyond the Pleasure Principle*. Translated by James Strachey. New York: W. W. Norton, 1975.

22. Freud, Sigmund. *Civilization and its Discontents*. Translated by James Strachey. New York: W. W. Norton, 1962.

23. Freud, Sigmund. *Collected Papers*. Translated by Joan Riviere. New York: Basic, 1959.

24. Freud, Sigmund. *New Introductory Lectures on Psychoanalysis.* Translated by James Strachey. New York: W. W. Norton, 1965.

25. Freud, Sigmund. *An Outline of Psychoanalysis.* Translated by James Strachey. New York: W. W. Norton, 1970.

26. Freud, Sigmund. *The Problem of Anxiety.* Translated by H. Bunker. New York: W. W. Norton, 1936.

27. Goethe, Johann W. *Goethe's World View.* Edited by Frederick Ungar. Translated by Heinz Norden. New York: Ungar, 1963.

28. Goldiamond, Israel. "Self-Control Procedures in Personal Behavior Problems." *Behavioral Change through Self-Control.* Edited by M. Goldfried and M. Merbaum. New York: Holt, Rinehart and Winston, 1973.

29. Gratten, Clinton Hartley. *The Three Jameses.* New York: New York University Press, 1962.

30. Guthrie, Edwin. *Psychology of Learning.* New York: Harper, 1935.

31. Guttman, N. "On Skinner and Hull." *American Psychologist,* 327, May, 1977.

32. Howard, K. and Orlansky, D. "Psychotherapeutic Processes." *Annual Review of Psychology,* 1972.

33. James, William. "The Dilemma of Determinism." *The Writings of William James.* Edited by J. McDermott. New York: Modern Library, 1968.

34. James, William. *Principles of Psychology.* New York: Dover, 1962.

35. James, William. *Talks to Teachers on Psychology and to Students on Some of Life's Ideals.* New York: W. W. Norton, 1958.

36. Jones, Ernest. *The Life and Work of Sigmund Freud.* New York: Basic, 1957.

37. Jung, Carl. *Two Essays on Analytical Psychology.* Princeton: Princeton University Press, 1972.

38. Keller, Fred S. and W. Schoenfeld. *Principles of Psychology.* New York: Irvington, 1950.

39. Koestler, Arthur. *The Ghost in the Machine.* New York: Macmillan, 1968.

40. Lazarus, A. A. "Where Do Behavioral Therapists Take Their Troubles?" *Psychology Reports,* 28, 349.

41. Lockard, R. "Reflections on the Fall of Comparative Psychology." *Readings in Animal Behavior.* Second edition. Edited by T. McGill. New York: Holt, Rinehart and Winston, 1973.

42. Lorenz, Konrad. *On Aggression.* New York: Harcourt, Brace, Jovanovich, 1966.

43. Meredith, Scott. *Writing to Sell.* New York: Harper and Row, 1974.

44. Pavlov, Ivan. *Conditioned Reflexes.* New York: Oxford University Press, 1927.

45. Peirce, Charles. *The Fixation of Belief.* New York: W. W. James. Westport, Connecticut: Greenwood, 1974.

46. Perry, Ralph B. *The Thought and Character of William* Norton, 1905.

47. Reich, Wilhelm. *Character Analysis.* Translated by Vincent Carfagno. New York: Farrar, Straus & Giroux, 1972.

48. Skinner, B. F. *Beyond Freedom and Dignity.* New York: Bantam, 1979.

49. Skinner, B. F. "Critique of Psychoanalytic Concepts and Theories." *Scientific Monthly,* 79, 300–305.

50. Skinner, B. F. *Science and Human Behavior.* New York: Irvington, 1979.

51. Smail, D. J. "The Therapeutic Community." *Issues and Approaches In The Psychological Therapies.* Edited by D. Bannister. London: Wiley and Sons, 1975.

52. Smith, Thomas Vernor. *Beyond Conscience.* New York: McGraw-Hill, 1934.

53. Sobell, M. and Sobell, L. *Behavior Therapy*, 4, 49–72.

54. Sullivan, Harry S. *Clinical Studies in Psychiatry*. New York: W. W. Norton, 1973.

55. Thompson, Clare Mabel. *Psychoanalysis: Evolution and Development*. New York: Grove, 1957.

56. Tillich, Paul. *The Courage to Be*. New Haven: Yale University Press, 1952.

57. Tindbergen, Niko. "On War and Peace in Animals and Man." *Readings in Animal Behavior*. Edited by Thomas McGill. New York: Holt, Rinehart and Winston, 1973.

58. Twain, Mark. *The Tragedy of Pudd'nhead Wilson*. Harmondsworth: Penguin, 1969.

59. Volkman, Rita and Cressy, Donald. "Differential Association and the Rehabilitation of Drug Addicts." *American Journal of Sociology*, 69, February, 1963.

60. Watson, John Broadus. *Behavior: An Introduction to Comparative Psychology*. New York: Holt, Rinehart and Winston, 1967.

61. Watson, John Broadus. *Behaviorism*. New York: W. W. Norton, 1970.

62. Weinberg, George. *The Action Approach*. New York: St. Martin's Press, 1969.

63. Weinberg, George. *Self Creation*. New York: St. Martin's Press, 1978.

64. Yates, Aubrey J. *Behavior Therapy*. New York: Wiley, 1970.

Index